MODES AND MORALS

MODES AND MORALS

BY

KATHARINE FULLERTON GEROULD

Essay Index Reprint Series

BOOKS FOR LIBRARIES PRESS
FREEPORT, NEW YORK

INTERNATIONAL STANDARD BOOK NUMBER:
0-8369-2317-0

LIBRARY OF CONGRESS CATALOG CARD NUMBER:
78-142634

PRINTED IN THE UNITED STATES OF AMERICA

CONTENTS

MODES AND MORALS

THE NEW SIMPLICITY

MY first caption was *Democracy, Plumbing, and the War*. That will hardly
do as a title, for it does not hint the
heart of the matter; though the war has pre-
cipitated conditions which our special form of
democracy has long been preparing us for, and
plumbing is perhaps as symbolic as it is ubiquit-
ous in the American domestic scene. All three,
with all their implications, are factors, certainly,
in our present problem of living, and if war
has brought that problem to acuteness, democracy and plumbing (and what they may be
taken to stand for) have made us ripe for up-
heaval. Edison and his like are as responsible,
in their way, as Thomas Jefferson or William
Haywood. All three have, without doubt, con-
tributed to the present and future dilemma of
educated people in moderate circumstances.
War has, of necessity, turned moderate circumstances to actual poverty; but democracy and
plumbing were already preparing the *débâcle*
for this group. All of us—the educated classes
as well as the uneducated—are guilty together,
that is, of pampering ourselves with physical
comforts; and democracy always makes for
materialism, because the only kind of equality

[3]

that you can guarantee to a whole people is, broadly speaking, physical. Democracy and plumbing, as well as war, make the problem of our immediate future a rather special one. We do not share all phases of it with our Allies. Let me explain, a little, what I mean.

If America has led the world in labor-saving devices, it is because America is democratic on a bigger scale than any other country. The person who profits by the labor-saving device is the person who does the work. The fact that France and England have not kept pace with us in plumbing and tiled kitchens and electrical appliances does not mean—as we have sometimes fatuously taken it to mean—that they are less civilized than we. It means only that personal service has been, with them, cheaper and more a matter of course. Where prosperous Americans multiply vacuum cleaners and electric washing machines and garbage incinerators, prosperous Europeans multiply their number of servants. The Englishman really prefers a huge tin tub in his bedroom of a morning. We prefer to walk into the bathroom and turn on the tap. That preference may well have become so natural that we cannot explain it. But the origin of the American preference is surely that in America only the very rich could afford a personal servant whose duty it was to set up the tub, fetch in huge cans of water, and remove all traces of the bath as soon as it was

[4]

done with. Even a few years ago, I remember having great difficulty in a London hotel of the better sort (but very English and almost totally unfrequented by Americans) in getting the chambermaid to procure me a slop-jar. The hotel was much too British to run to numbers of private baths. Hence the crying need of a slop-jar. The maid finally stole one for me from a room across the corridor, and assured me that the gentleman from whom she stole would not miss it. Nothing would induce her to resume, in his behalf, the treasure. I am informed, by friends who have more British social experience than I, that slop-jars are not in the best English tradition—because, theoretically, in the opulent old-fashioned household, as soon as you have washed your hands, the water in which you washed them, the towel on which you wiped them, mysteriously and gracefully disappear. Perfection of service lies in having plenty of dexterous servants lying in wait to discover your needs; so many servants, and such well-trained ones, that you cannot wash your hands without their becoming aware of it and, with the least possible impinging on your notice, removing the traces of your ablutions. Perfection of service does not involve your emptying your own wash-basin, even into a slop-jar. Hence, no slop-jar.

Now there are very few of us who would take the trouble to invent a tiled bathroom if

[5]

our tubs were automatically fetched, filled, and removed for us, all at the proper instant; or if a hot-water can miraculously sprang into being as soon as the desire for hot water seized us. There is no labor-saving device so perfectly convenient as ringing a bell and having some one else do the thing for you with complete competence. It is by no means strange that well-to-do Europeans have been content to be supremely waited upon, instead of making practical tasks mechanically easier for themselves. The goddess of the labor-saving invention is the woman who does all, or a good share, of "her own work." Old-fashioned English and French houses are cold; but (climate apart) nothing like so cold as American houses would be if Americans depended on open fires. For in England or France there are ten people to make the fires, to one in America. We simply dare not—again, climate apart— depend, as our British cousins have been wont to, on open fires. The average household cannot afford the servants to do incessant fire-making all over the house.

So we have multiplied devices, from the modest kitchen cabinet up; because that majority which advertisers and inventors are always trying to reach does a lot of things for itself. Even those Americans who always have had, and perhaps still will have, plenty of servants, have indulged in these devices. For pure philanthropy's sake? Well, I am afraid not quite. Rather, because the standard having been set by the mistress who is also the servant, the standard must be lived up to, or professional servants would complain. The interesting point is that in America the standard is set by the woman who does her own work or a part of it, or who may, at any given moment, have to occupy herself thus. We are, you see, a democracy beyond the democracies of other lands. For it is not simply a question of money; it is a question of our all being in the same boat.

I am not going into the servant question, for that is a question as trite as it is tragic. But, as we all know, even before the war it was growing acute. The best servants we had in the old days came from the countries where personal service was a tradition—chiefly from the territories of Great Britain. But northern Europe is ceasing to enter domestic service; rather, it seeks to employ. One has only to read the pathetic testimony in the daily press, in the "women's magazines," even sometimes in philanthropic periodicals. What they all say is that the only way you can keep your cook in your kitchen is to treat her as if she were the governess, or to give her factory hours and factory freedom—to put her on a level, that is, with the more independent worker. At that, they do not give us much hope of keeping her. But I fancy that, before we turn the whole house over to the cook, we shall dispense with her and get our meals from co-operative kitchens.

I have noticed of late years in the magazines that deal with architectural and decorative problems increasing stress on the absurdity of having a dining-room. Why absurd? For only one reason: that here is a room which must be cleaned, which, therefore, means more service. If you have your meals in the "living-room," you dispense with so much floor-and-wall space to be gone over. In only that sense is it absurd. For most of us will agree that while English lodgings are all very well, especially for a solitary creature, it is a painful business for a large family to eat three meals a day in a room which has to be lived in otherwise. All people may not have the prejudice known to some of us against social consumption of food; but any one will agree that the best dinner in the world leaves a smell behind it. A dining-room may be a luxury, but it is not an absurdity, so long as you can by any means afford it. If the æsthetic and pseudo-æsthetic experts in domesticity are telling us that a dining-room is ridiculous, it is only because they wish to prepare us for an inevitable contraction of our comfort, an unavoidable mitigation of decency. The one most aristocratic element in life, physically speaking, is spaciousness; it has always been in the best

[8]

tradition to be frugal to starvation in a corner of a palace. But we have come nowadays to care more for what we eat (I fear) than for how or where we eat it. The abolition of the dining-room is only a further step on the road we entered when we moved *en masse* out of houses into flats. It has been hard to get service; and meanwhile we have grown soft and would rather do without those amenities which are not conveniences than to furnish them for ourselves.

It must in fairness be admitted that two things have combined to bring us to this pass. The most obvious fact is this of the labor situation, which is now immensely accentuated by the war. But another force has always been at work. Except in that part of the country which imported slaves early and kept them as long as it could, more or less pioneer standards prevailed. We were a new country; we dispensed perforce (as in other colonies) with many of the inherited comforts. Our love of personal (I do not mean political) independence was a kind of protective coloring. The enforced simplicity of the pioneer scene bred in us a distaste for being waited on too importunately. Because we had to do certain things for ourselves, we developed a preference for doing them, a distaste for the constant interposition of another human being among the more private processes of existence. Even in the South, some modifica-

[9]

tion of the tradition must have been necessary, for the South must always have been badly, though exuberantly, served. Here and there a butler, a lady's maid, may, after years of struggle, have been highly trained; and the colored race has a gift for cooking. But in many ways Southerners must have contended with the disheartening conditions faced by all English households in the outposts of empire, dependent on another and a stupid race for the satisfaction of their needs. Southern luxury lay in having a score of inadequate menials to keep the masters as comfortable as three or four really good servants would have done. It was slave labor, and slave labor reaches competence only by sheer force of numbers. There was never an ideal of domestic service there, because there was never the rounded conception of civilized domestic comfort in any slave's mind. And nothing is more slovenly or incompetent in domestic service than the younger generation of free-born negroes. I do not think the colored race is going to prove our domestic salvation.

We welcomed the labor-saving device, in the first place, for the reasons I have given. By the labor-saving device we have been brought insensibly to an almost animal dependence on creature comforts. With all our theoretical glorification of simplicity, we have really prided ourselves supremely on our physical luxuries, and most of all, it must be said, on those physical luxuries which have no æsthetic value. Our plumbing has been our civilization. The European aristocracy is for the most part not so "comfortable" as the American middle class; and therefore we have considered ourselves the greatest nation in the world. We have been snobbish about many things, but about nothing so much as our electrical appliances and our skyscrapers. We have sinned, all of us together, as I said before; and now we are paying. Simplicity, austerity, even, are forced upon us; and it behooves those of us who really care, in spite of temporary apostasies, about real values, to take thought and to plan. The vital question is not whether we shall simplify, but how. On that depends our civilization.

Neither the new war millionaires nor skilled labor can teach us that. We shall have need of all our trained perceptions, of all our first-hand and all our book knowledge, of what money has been most wisely spent for in the past, to make our choice intelligently. The new millionaire and the enriched laboring man will not, for the most part, be able to help us; for, by and large, having no experience of the finer things of civilization, they will not know. For ourselves, it does not much matter—for us who have seen a world in ruin and can never "care" for anything in the same way again—

but this is perhaps our first duty to our children. They cannot have all the things we were brought up to crave and expect; but they must have the essentials. What, in a practical sense, are those going to be?

The Pennsylvania miner, making from forty to seventy-five dollars a day, buys an automobile—not necessarily a Ford—which waits for him at the entrance to the mine. His wife buys finery. Both buy the best food they can get. It has been publicly said, I understand, by a distinguished representative of the Food Administration, that almost every class of the community was doing its duty in the way of food conservation, except skilled labor. That is the class which cannot be reached by appeal. The very poorest are still very poor, and they have neither the money nor the knowledge to enable them to indulge in forbidden gastronomic luxuries. The rich are apparently—in most cases—making it a point of honor to help out. But skilled labor, which is so necessary to the prosecution of war, which has never in its life been so pampered, so flattered, so kowtowed to, so overpaid (yes, I mean that; it is overpaid, and I will explain what I mean presently), has lost its head. It probably believes the things the politicians and its own leaders have been saying to it. It will work, and consider itself patriotic for working—but it will exact from the rest of us, the public, a price it has no right to, and, lest the honor of our country and the ideals we fight for be lost, we shall pay it. It may be that the reckoning will come later; or it may be that we are so sunk in materialism that skilled labor will continue to rule the earth. Just so long as we feel our greatest need to be of the things it furnishes us with, and its greatest need is for the things we cannot furnish it with, our necks will be bowed under labor's yoke. Our only chance of emancipation lies in finding some of our greatest goods in fields not under labor's control. In other words, to live at all, in any peace, in any equanimity and longanimity, we must be as little materialistic in temper and desire as possible. We must teach our children that the greatest goods are not the things that skilled labor produces. That is not only truth; it is self-preservation. Labor will have the motorcars and the delicacies of the table, the jewels and the joy-rides; we must see to it that we keep something else, and learn to feel the importance of our treasure. If we can maintain a prestige value for the things of our choice (frankly, I doubt if we can) "the lords of their hands" may come to desire the things we have chosen, and help to make them accessible. But we must be careful to make no concessions; we must not take one step, ourselves, in the materialistic direction.

This is not snobbishness; it is a matter of

life and death. No one is going to have leisure, any more, to be a snob or any such non-essential thing. At least, if any one has the time, it will not be the educated classes. We shall have to work as we have never worked before, physically as well as mentally. We shall have to learn to co-operate with one another, too; to make an almost religious brotherhood. For it is our children who matter, and we cannot begin too soon to prepare them for a world which has nothing in common with the world we knew. Only by joining in utmost effort with the like-minded can we hope to protect them.

I know there are Utopians who see in the socialization of Anglo-Saxon governments hope, along Marxian lines, for Anglo-Saxondom. They foresee, I suppose, the kind of Paradise that the Admirable Crichton (in Barrie's immoral and delightful play) must have experienced on the desert island. There is going to be only one party in England, Mr. Arthur Henderson has recently said—the Labor party. It may be. Let us hope that some of the "unattached leaders" will at least preserve logic if they do not preserve majorities. Mr. Henderson's own argument is about as convincing as though one should say: in certain abnormal conditions martial law is the only régime that will work; therefore, since civil law has been found inadequate to conditions of riot and pestilence and famine, we must give it up altogether, and make martial law perpetual.

[14]

The real arguments against private, and for public, ownership are, of course, quite other than those Mr. Henderson offers. The point is that Mr. Henderson evidently does not know bad logic when he sees it. Let Mr. Henderson and his followers keep the motor-cars, one is inclined to say, and we will keep the logic he discards. Private perception of the laws of logic is something we shall not be taxed for; though—let us not deceive ourselves—we shall have to make sacrifices to keep it. If we can acquire logic, we may have it. It may be increasingly difficult to maintain the methods of acquiring it: the best education, moral and intellectual, was becoming endangered before the war, and there is no telling what may become of it afterward.

I seem to have wandered far afield from plumbing; and yet plumbing (as a symbol of materialistic comfort) is more than germane to the question. The group whose problem I am concerned with is a very large one, though always, anywhere, a minority: the professional man, the man in the smaller business position, the man on a salary, who has been decently bred, and who can never look forward to any real financial fortune. I do not include every one who has to economize strictly, for a large proportion of the people who have to economize strictly are totally uneducated as to real values. But distinctly I include any of the last mentioned who are alive to something besides materialistic needs. I do not include the people who want intellectual and æsthetic goods only for social and snobbish reasons or out of blind jealousy. That group, in any case, will cease to exist if intellectual and æsthetic goods cease to have a social value—as is more and more definitely coming to be the case. They were never anything but paid mercenaries in the struggle.

How are we going to save, for our children and our children's children, the real amenities of life? Hitherto the new millionaires, for reasons of social prestige, have tended to link themselves to the group of the civilized. But the new millionaire has always been an individual case, and has, therefore, had to make concessions to the group already established. What we have never had before is the proletariat suddenly becoming, overnight, in its vast numbers, at once richer and more powerful politically than the little "educated" aristocracy. We all know what happens when that happens; if we have forgotten the French Revolution (and since 1914 a good many of us have) we have the Russian Revolution to remind us. In this morning's newspaper I saw that the daily bread ration in Petrograd was one-half a pound for the proletariat, one-eighth of a pound for the bourgeoisie. That may or may not be true, but there is nothing in known facts to make it incredible. Even granting that skilled labor is not going to Bolshevize itself completely, there is no doubt that the minority of which I speak is going to be virtually, if not theoretically, discriminated against. Labor is not going to draw distinctions between employers of labor; the college professor is going to have to pay the plumber, the carpenter, at as exorbitant rates as the great manufacturer. Any one who employs labor at all—even if it is only to repair a leak—is going to be gouged. All along the line, the producers of every necessary element in civilized physical existence are going to rob the ultimate consumer. It is labor that is responsible for the high cost of living. Labor may say that the high cost of living is responsible for its increased demands. In point of fact, there is every evidence that labor at present is demanding money, not for the necessities of life, but for the luxuries— just like the capitalists they have so inveighed against. One would have to be a professional reformer to be shocked. Any knowledge of human nature leaves one perfectly unsurprised by this phenomenon. Most men have always wanted as much as they could get; and possession has always blunted the fine edge of their altruism. That is what labor has always said about the employers of labor; and the employers can say it quite as truly of the employed. So long as you make the basis of life materialistic, this law will prevail.

[17]

What, then, are we going to do about it?
We shall not be able to afford many of the
luxuries we once thought necessities, and we
must decide, with the utmost possible wisdom,
what are necessities and what are not. We had
better make our list as short as possible, at
that. Obvious luxuries we shall not have:
motor-cars, fine clothing, plenty of domestic
service, the joys of travel. It is costing us more,
all the time, to provide the hygienic necessities
for our children: pure milk, nourishing food,
good air, healthful recreation, seasonable clothing. I do not mean complicated food, or extravagant amusements, or elaborate clothing;
I mean the irreducible minimum required for
health and simple comfort and decency. And
we cannot all—especially the professional people—go back to the farm and live on our own
produce. We have to struggle along as best we
can in the communities to which our work has
called us.

In some ways the life of the spirit and the
life of the intellect have always been expensive.
The more obvious material comforts—rich
food, for example—have not been necessary to
either. Neither, in a sense, has fine clothing or
expensive furniture. Yet it must be remembered that both the life of the spirit and the
life of the intellect tend, in most cases, to
develop the sense of beauty; and that too much
ugliness can become a pain and an obstacle to

calm. There is a simplicity that is pleasing, and a simplicity that is hideous. Leaving aside the social importance of good clothes and good furniture, there is, in downright ugliness, a power to fret the soul, a power to lessen the power to work. But we will neglect, for the moment, the æsthetic side of it. In the matter of food we will willingly simplify. In the matter of adornment, whether of our persons or of our houses, we shall have to simplify, and we can only hope that our simplification can be conducted more along quantitative than along qualitative lines. We shall try to omit rather than commit; to be austere rather than cheap.

The matter of servants is going to hit us harder; for only with "help"—in the quite literal sense—can we manage to get any peace or any time, in the hours left free by our wage-earning, for reading, for contemplation, for conversation. The "general houseworker" has tended to disappear; which is an acknowledgment that when a great many different things have to be done, one human being cannot stand the strain. Only by her being helped out by the family, only by some features of household service being scanted or ill done, could the general houseworker ever manage to keep outside her job. The good cook could not also be the perfect parlor-maid and the perfect child's nurse. Neither can the good physician, the good lawyer, the good clergyman, also be the perfect choreman, the perfect gardener, and the perfect butler—with hours of casual bookkeeping, plumbing, and carpentering. Even if he had the talent, he would not have the time; for the physician, the lawyer, and the clergyman are not safeguarded by an "eight-hour day." His wife, moreover, even if she has no private intellectual interests, cannot suffice to all the modern domestic tasks any more than can the general houseworker, who has faded out of existence precisely because she could not. We shall modify as we can; shall have our food sent in from outside where that is possible; shall buy vacuum cleaners (on the instalment plan); shall win occasional hours of freedom by hiring some safe person to come in and watch over the children while they sleep. Hospitality will, of necessity, be much curtailed. Our personal freedom—in any familiar sense of the term—will be almost *nil.* We might defy our house, our garden, our table, our door-bell, to shackle us; but we cannot defy our children to shackle us.

In these ways, we shall probably intrigue for the life of the spirit, the life of the intellect. But, still, they are expensive. Education—good education—is, in the first place, expensive. I do not know how much it costs to make a man a good plumber or a good coal-miner or a good carpenter; but I am sure it does not cost so much as it does to make him a good doctor or a good clergyman. It takes seven years after the "prep" school or the high school to start the professional man on his road, costing fairly heavily all the time. That is why I said that skilled labor is overpaid—it gets an exorbitant return for its expenditure. Most of us hope to have college for our boys, even if they do not take up a profession—just because we think that education is going to matter to a man, all his life, no matter in what field he works. The joys of travel, as I intimated, are going to be cut out for most of us; the opera and the play will become infrequent blessings. But we shall have to have some books—even if we do not start the furnace until December. Indeed, the books we have ourselves are perhaps going to be our best guarantee of our children's being educated at all. To be sure, we shall be taxed on them, with increasing heaviness; but then, the coal-miner will (let us hope) be taxed on his motor-car.

It may be that we shall come to state-endowed motherhood, and all the rest. But the trouble is that all these socialistic schemes are based on a lower-class demand on life. State endowment of motherhood will perhaps have to come; but what does it guarantee except the child born under decent conditions? The health of the mother, and through her of the child, is to be safeguarded. Very well. *Et après?* Pure milk may be provided at municipal stations; there will be a day nursery and then a public kindergarten. There will follow — if modern "educators" have their way — the whole desolating career in the public schools, where real education is reduced to a minimum, and "vocational" training is substituted. The child will, in time, be graduated into the ranks of skilled labor, and perhaps will eventually have his motor-car and his tiled bathroom and his "movie" every night.

Yet for some of us this is not a supremely cheering prospect, because it is a wholly materialistic vision. Certainly it is a good thing to start with health as a requisite. Certainly everything that can be done to insure a healthy childhood, in every case where it is physically possible, should be done. But the great mistake of the reformers is to believe that life begins and ends with health, and that happiness begins and ends with a full stomach and the power to enjoy physical pleasures, even of the finer kind. It may be that the enormous expense of guaranteeing health to all children born in our vast American community will take all the money that the community has. It may be that no one will ever be free to devote his health to pursuing the life of the mind and the spirit— to the purposes, that is, of civilization not purely physical. But we have not come to that yet; and the war is there to remind us that we really do not know precisely what will come.

If real socialism—as distinguished from our temporary utilization of certain socialistic methods—comes, we shall inevitably turn our backs on civilization for a time. Successful socialism depends on the perfectibility of man. Unless all, or nearly all, men are high-minded and clear-sighted, it is bound to be a rotten failure in any but a physical sense. Even though it is altruism, socialism means materialism. You can guarantee the things of the body to every one, but you cannot guarantee the things of the spirit to every one; you can guarantee only that the opportunity to seek them shall not be denied to any one who chooses to seek them. And socialism, believing as it must (to hold its head high) in the spiritual as well as the political equality of men, is not going to create special opportunities for the special case. "To hell with the special case" is implicit in the socialist slogan. Do you see any majority, anywhere, in this imperfect and irreligious world, admitting that the minority is precious? That any minority is precious? Is there any evidence whatever that the socialist is less avid of personal political power, less averse to demagogic methods, than the other person? Does he himself go far to prove his perfectionism? A good many socialists are calling other socialists names because they put nationality before internationality; though any one with any sense could have told them beforehand that they would,

because human beings are—fortunately or unfortunately — like that. Lenin and Trotzky
are disappointed because the German socialists
do not rise to betray their rulers; and some
socialists are disappointed because Lenin and
Trotzky appear to be selling Russia out to
Germany in order to keep themselves—two
individuals—in places of power. Every one is
calling names all round; and if socialism were
anything in particular, it would (one would
think) be very sorry for itself.

What is clear is this: that the socialization
of governments places vast power in the hands
of the skilled laborer. It is only in order that
labor shall produce as fast and as furiously as
possible that we have socialized our national
organization. We need, chiefly for war's sake,
certain physical things—food, munitions, coal,
khaki clothing, and transportation for the
same. We are calling for Y. M. C. A. men,
and K. of C., and chaplains; but what we
really expect of them, more than anything else,
is to go under fire, if necessary, to give the soldiers tobacco and hot chocolate. The newspapers lay eager and delighted stress on the
unclerical nature of the services these gentlemen find themselves cheerfully performing.
War, you see, is a physical business. Of the
spiritual side of it I am not going to speak. No
one really can speak of it in terms of actual
achievement until the armies have come home

and we see what manner of men they are. You cannot tell from the straws you see which way the great last wind of all is going to blow. Some wise people doubt whether the veterans of this war are going to spiritualize the world. Many of them will have had, at this or that supreme moment, something akin to a spiritual revelation. But the spiritual adventure is a desperately and exclusively personal thing; you cannot socialize it. It is incommunicable, and for the most part inexpressible. The attempt to socialize a spiritual experience ends in the camp-meeting; it goes no farther. Like all mental ecstasies, it cannot be felt simultaneously by millions of people. I fancy that the opinions the veterans are going to express at the polls are quite unforeknowable. We are all willingly kow-towing to the materialists for the sake of the armies. Whether the armies will wish to kow-tow to them when the war is over is a question more difficult of present solution than the Balkan boundaries. Certainly, if the armies have developed an *esprit de corps* and a philosophy of their own, they will be listened to. We shall inevitably be very sentimental about them. Whether we shall continue to be sentimental about the man who selected this moment to hold up his country and his compatriots for exorbitant pay, and demonstrated his patriotism by earning it, I do not know. We can deal only with the present situation.

What, the present outlook being what it is, can we count on for our children? We shall be practically aided, in time, as I have said, by all sorts of co-operative schemes—invented for the use of the very poor, and adapted and expanded, of necessity, for the not quite so poor. Some of the amenities of life, some of the space and the privacy, will have gone irretrievably. After considerations of health come considerations of education. We shall not be able, probably, to afford private schools for our children; and our sole comfort must be that most private schools are not much good, anyhow. They are a little safer gamble, in most communities, than the public schools. That is all. We, the parents, must supplement the bad teaching as best we can, must keep at least some spark of intelligent interest in the universe alive by the gas-log. It may well become our painful and subversive duty to inform our children, from the beginning, that what is being offered them by the state as education is not really education at all; and that teaching a boy how to make bookshelves is in no sense a substitute for teaching him to read and appreciate Latin. (Better not mention Greek!) It is very desirable, if not absolutely necessary, for our daughter to know how to cook; but we must not permit her to consider that domestic science is education, in the proper sense. We must keep the fact before ourselves and before the next generation that the training of the mind does not mean quite the same thing as the training of the muscles. Time was when a cobbler—and I do not mean anything so remote and legendary as Hans Sachs—found philosophy a very natural complement to cobbling. I knew a cobbler in my childhood who was much in demand among the intellectuals, as being one of the few people who could expound Emerson's transcendentalism in a completely satisfactory way. He went about— I can still recall the spun snow of his hair, the canny saintliness of his much-modelled face, the thin figure under the long black cloak — to philosophical conferences, to discuss metaphysics with the metaphysicians; and returned to sit in his little shop and cobble shoes. But one has yet to hear of philosophy's coming from a member of the lasters' union. Machinery means specialization; and it is an old story that there is no mental comfort or development in repeating the same gesture for eight hours a day, even if one has time and a half for overtime. The single gesture is not educative. When you saw the shoe as an entity, when it grew under your hands and you built up the whole consciously from the related parts; even when you were a mere cobbler, a physician to sick shoes, and had to know the whole shoe-organism— there was something in that humblest, most physical of tasks which demanded a conception

in the brain. That time is gone, and if William
Morris in the flesh could not bring it back,
certainly his ghost will not. But if you think
for a moment of the difference in mental attitude and mental grasp, it shows up skilled
labor for what it is.

I am far from saying that, in this much
simpler world which the increasing complica-
tion of life is going, paradoxically, to create
for some of us, it is a bad thing that children
should be "vocationally" trained. (You cannot
say "vocationally educated," for that is virtually a contradiction in terms.) Even so, it is
only to a very limited degree that our sons can
be, in the intervals, their own plumbers or
their own carpenters or their own masons, for
the unions will never allow it. It is a very
minor tinkering that is permitted to the private
person. You cannot help to paint your own
woodwork in your own house, for the union
painter will leave his job if you touch your
private paint-brush in his presence. What good,
after all, is this famous vocational training,
except as you definitely choose to follow
through life some one of the trades they teach
you? It will not really make the whole man
more efficient; for he will not be allowed to
use his potential efficiency. It may teach him
whether he prefers to be a steamfitter or a
bricklayer; but it cannot guarantee him any
power to practise either steamfitting or brick-

laying, unless he is willing to forsake all else and cling only to that. Never was such nonsense talked by any one as by the new "educators." Labor frankly uses the argument of might and the big stick; but labor, as far as I know, does not pretend that it is something else. It rests its case cynically on our own pampered inability to get on without it.

"Philosophy can bake no bread," replied some philosopher to his critics, "but it can give us God, freedom, and immortality." Those are the last things, I take it, that modern philosophy is really concerned with giving us; but the perversity of one generation need not obscure all history. It is possible for the contemplation of great ideas, of great art, of great poetry, of the epic motions of the human race as revealed in history, to mitigate physical deprivation. It is possible to have plain living and high thinking together—though it is not easy, and never has been, and some of the best-known exponents of that theory have been pitiful failures. Certainly we of the minority must accept for ourselves austerities we were not bred to in our easy-going, materialistic generation. Without taking, like St. Simeon, to the wilful discomfort of a pillar, we must learn to do without a hundred "necessities" that Dante and Shakespeare never dreamed of. We must keep it possible for our children to delight in Dante and Shakespeare; we must not let the authentic intellectual thrill disappear from the world. And, for that, we must insist that the past be not closed to them, and that learning shall not be an unknown good. They will have to do it on bread and milk, not on caviare; but it can be done on bread and milk. That is the point.

I confess that as I look forth in these distressed times on the vast American scene, I find myself pinning my hope to two things— the self-consciousness of this minority, and the older Eastern universities. For unless we plan our simplicities cannily, the other people will have won out; and unless the older universities keep up a standard of learning, hold the door open, by main force, to the past, the garnered lore of the world will fail us. We shall progress —but blindly, as the brute creation. The fact is that we are living in an obscurantist epoch. For surely it is obscurantism to deny the legitimacy of any field of knowledge or of virtue, and those folk who would reduce everything to a physical basis are as deadly foes of light as their ancestors who saw in physical experiments nothing but the black art. Every sane person wants science left free to accomplish its marvellous work; but no sane person past early youth would say, as a young woman fresh from her college laboratories said to me a few days since, that chemistry is the root of all knowledge. The Protestants, when they were on top, were as given to obscurantism, and its accompaniment of persecution, as the Catholics.

In the matter of education, as I have suggested, we shall have to rely on the older colleges of the East. We cannot count on the West to help us, for the West is cursed with state universities. It is by no means my intention or my private inclination to minimize the value of the state universities. The point is that they are uncertain; they are not free; they are dependent, in the last analysis, on public favor, which means public funds, on a kind of initiative and referendum. They may have good luck and become great schools of learning; they may have bad luck and become indifferent and negligible places. They are not really allowed to set their own standards; they must ever be compromising with the personnel of state legislatures. The private colleges and universities of the East at least are not dependent on politics. Their funds are for the most part inadequate, but they do not have to change their curricula to please people who know nothing about what a curriculum should be. As long as their private fortunes last, they can afford to say the thing which they believe to be true. One of the most heartening things that have happened since 1914 is the acquisition of great wealth by Yale University. It means—one hopes—that one at least of our

[31]

old academic foundations can snap its fingers at ignorance enthroned; that it can send out its thousands endowed with some sense of intellectual values. Intellectual values are not the only ones; but most sane people believe that only by the rigid training of the mind can human beings be taught wise living and moral values. There is no morality by instinct, though there can be morality by inherited inhibitions. There is no social salvation—in the end—without taking thought; without mastery of logic and application of logic to human experience. These things, because they are not the natural man, are not carelessly come by; they must be deliberately achieved. You will not learn them from the Bolsheviki, or from the I. W. W., or even from Mr. Arthur Henderson. A great deal is said nowadays about practical politics and the rôle of the practical man in building the social structure. Before you can carry out an idea you must have the idea. You cannot get rid of the world of abstract thought. One after the other, leaders of the Church are laying more and more stress on religion's being a strictly social matter. Perhaps it is, though I do not believe it. I should have said that social regeneration was a by-product of religion, not religion itself. But even the folk who think that Christianity means no slums, and means little else, derive their sanction—or think they do—from Christ, who dealt in abstract ideas more exclusively than any other religious teacher the world has had.

We must, then, seriously facing the moral, political, and physical conditions of our time, be frankly ascetic. We must make our children healthy, first of all—if only because specialists will be beyond our pocketbooks. I have implied that the combination of plain living and high thinking is a difficult one; I fancy it is the most difficult in the world. "The hand of little employment hath the daintier sense." We shall obliterate the coarser contacts, as far as possible, not by engaging other people to take the burden of those coarser contacts, but by buying, as we can, the machinery that will suffice to them impersonally. We shall "co-operate" to the limit of our incomes, losing thereby, I repeat, many of the amenities which tend to civilize. We shall not sleep soft, we shall not live high, and we shall do without external beauty to a painful extent. We shall exist in cramped quarters, and if we achieve the dignity of one spacious room, that will be a great deal. We cannot hope to furnish it fittingly. But if we have a dollar to spend on some wild excess, we shall spend it on a book, not on asparagus out of season. If we have a holiday, we shall not go to Europe or Asia, which would be beyond our means; but we shall find some quiet spot where there will at least be

[33]

trees and sky and no motor-cars or aeroplanes. We shall, I hope, ameliorate our lack of space and privacy by a very perfectly developed courtesy and by the capacity for silence. It sounds monastic, and, at its best, monastic it will be. Certain things we shall have given up at the start; certain ambitions will have been erased from our tablets. We shall not compete with, or interfere with, the lords of this world. We shall do our modest work, and receive our modest pay, and by a corresponding modesty of life and temper we shall disarm, we hope, the unsympathetic and uncomprehending. Our kingdom cannot be of this world; and instead of complaining and criticizing, we must apply ourselves to realizing that our compensations can be made greater than our losses. We shall be passionately concerned with humanity; the more so, that we shall endeavor to be aware of the voice of God as well as of the voice of the people. We shall not be snobs in any sense; for we shall have the same charity for other people's choices that we beg them to have for ours. Besides, snobbishness dies out quickly— in America, at least—among the impoverished.

Even those who find all this an intolerable idea will dub it Utopian. A counsel of perfection it certainly is. But the higher the standard we set for ourselves the less likely we are to put up with a low one. And if we merely drift, I fear we shall find ourselves getting nothing—

[34]

wearing ourselves out in the unequal, familiar race for physical privileges, and leaving to one side the intangible goods. We can guarantee our children nothing except that they shall be armored against certain kinds of suffering; the lust of non-essentials, for example. I do not say that we shall not lose much that our best interest would suggest our having; but we shall not lose everything. And with the new simplicity will come some of the compensations of earlier simplicity. The man who has three things gets more pleasure out of one than does the man who has a hundred. Perhaps we shall capture the "joy in widest commonalty spread." A rose will always be cheaper than an alligator pear, and it is quite possible to enjoy it as much and as vividly. We shall be very grateful, I have no doubt, to Thomas Edison and the other genii of democracy. In some ways we shall fare better than folk of our clan in Europe. We must thank our stars for plumbing —itself a "joy in widest commonalty spread." But we shall value it chiefly as it releases time for better things, and those better things not physical pleasures.

Not only shall we not glorify our plumbing with marble; we shall see that there is really no sense in marble when porcelain will do as well—that marble has better uses and should be kept for them. Not only shall we have no ermine to shield us from the cold; we shall see that ermine was more beautiful when rarely and ritually worn. We shall learn to take pleasure in beautiful things that do not and never can belong to us; and we shall purge ourselves of the ignoble passion of envy. But the power to discriminate between the truth and a lie—which is the foundation of all moral and intellectual enjoyment—we shall cling to with greed. For in keeping that we rob no one, and insult no law. I am far from believing that any group of people can achieve all this with completeness. But I believe we shall do well to set it before us as a goal.

DRESS AND THE WOMAN

THE creed and the fallacy of fashion, it seems to me, have seldom been better expressed than in the retort once made to a friend of mine, in one of our more conservative New England towns. Sojourning there for a time, she had reason to order a hat from a local milliner. When she tried it on, it did not resemble in the least the headgear of the metropolis. "They are wearing hats very low, this year, you know," she protested. "Ah," was the unperturbed reply, "they are wearing them high in Newburyport." I do not remember the fate of the hat—which is unimportant; but the statement has remained with me for years as one of the most significant imaginable. It was at once the glorification and the *reductio ad absurdum* of modishness. My friend and the milliner spoke in the same spirit. For provincialism in dress consists merely in adhering rigidly to the *avant-dernier cri*. The object of allegiance may be, in the provinces, a little tardily come up with; but the rigidity is precisely the rigidity of the rue de la Paix. Fashion is not simply a question of longitude.

The sense of mode might be considered, as so many other things have been, the possession that distinguishes man from the beasts. The peacock is no proof to the contrary; for if, as scientists suggest to us, all radiant plumage has been developed as a means of attraction, at least the ideal of adornment has been, in the case of the birds, consistently æsthetic. The feathery fashions have always been intrinsically good. Whereas (to be flippant) the attraction exercised by the latest mode would seem usually to point to some principle of unnatural selection. The bird of Paradise, who is probably irresistible in his native forest, can be positively repellent on a hat. Yes; the sense of mode is curiously different from the sense of beauty. Let us, however, be serious.

Preachers of all time—and satirists, who are lay-preachers — have declaimed against female extravagance in dress. It must be confessed that the sex of the more peaceful pursuits has been the more exuberantly adorned. The male costume worn, say, at the court of Henri III, was every bit as bad as anything that contemporary ladies could have boasted; but even in the time of Henri III, a man had to hold himself ready for the saddle and the tented field. Some part of his life was bound to be spent in garments as rational as he could conceive them. It was the female sex that could expand, unchecked and unpruned, into such wild tendrils, such orchid-like incontinent bloom, of "changeable apparel."

From the earliest times, it is the woman who has been designated as the sinner in this respect. On this point, the Old and New Testaments are, for once, agreed; Isaiah and St. Paul are at one. "The chains, and the bracelets, and the mufflers, the bonnets . . . and the earrings . . . the mantles, and the wimples, and the crisping-pins . . . the fine linen, and the hoods and the veils," the one accuses; "broidered hair, or gold, or pearls, or costly array," complains the other. Ezekiel thunders against "the women that sew pillows to the armholes" (the *gigot* sleeve in the reign of Zedekiah!) "and make kerchiefs for the head of persons of every stature, to hunt souls." And the tradition has remained. It is perhaps the only subject on which St. Ignatius Loyola and John Knox would have been thoroughly sympathetic. One is certainly at liberty to infer from the chorus that it is easier for a camel to pass through the needle's eye than for anything really *chic* to enter the Kingdom of Heaven.

All these gentlemen, to be sure, seem to have objected to the fact and purpose of feminine adornment, rather than to rapid changes in the methods adopted. But I cannot believe that St. Paul, who scored the Attic curiosity born of the Attic *ennui,* would not have preached even more violently, had he foreseen the need, against fashion than against beauty. And is it not fashion rather than beauty that

[39]

is subtly discriminated against by all religious orders? The nun, like the Quakeress, must adopt a single color and a single mode; though nun and Quakeress, both, often find their chosen garb the most becoming they could possibly wear. No dress could be more beautiful than that which I remember from my childhood's convent. It fell in rich and simple folds of *violet*—*violet* being neither purple nor crimson, but something indefinably magnificent midway between — enhanced by white linen *guimpe* and cream-colored veiling. It gave the daughter of a French duke, I remember, the aspect of a queen regnant. Yet it represented poverty, chastity, and obedience. No one is especially concerned with the nun's being unbecomingly clad. A subtler mortification is supposed to lie in her engaging to dress in exactly the same way all her life. The mortification is of course heightened by the fact that she shares her style of dress with the rest of the community, regardless of type. But in any case the first thing that the postulant renounces is fashionable clothing. They leave her curls to be cut off later.

It is not, however, with the moral aspect of fashion that I am concerned. The moral question, indeed, has ceased to be very poignant; even our Calvinist great-grandmothers permitted a shy predominance of trimming on the "congregation side" of their bonnets. The

moral aspect of fashion disguises itself nowadays as an economic consideration. With economic considerations, again, I have no special
concern. They are writ large over half the
printed pages of our time. Some statistician
every month proves to us something appalling:
either that,

   . . . since our women must walk gay, and money buys
their gear,

materials are adulterated, or sewing-women
are starved, or shop-girls seek the primrose
path, or husbands die of the strain in their early
forties. To much the same music, the New
York Customs officials stage, each day, an
elaborate melodrama on the steamship piers.
We know that, from "Nearseal" to "Near-
silk," the poor will sacrifice comfort to cut, and
that a really "good" milliner makes a profit of
a hundred per cent on each hat. These things
are all true; and Heaven forbid that one
should shirk the economic question! But I very
much doubt if either moralist or statistician
will turn the trick. Yet they have only, it would
seem, to enlist a few other facts as good as
their own, to be quite sure of success.

For not even the cynic will pretend that the
real object of fashions is to disfigure. It is
quite without intention that M. Worth and
Mme. Paquin and all their prototypes, con-
geners, and successors, have become the foes

of beauty. They have simply never stopped to consider that the very notion of the changing mode is the negation of all æsthetic law. The most damning thing about fashions is that they make inevitably, nine years out of ten, for the greatest ugliness of the greatest number. And this is the real Achilles tendon of *la mode*. Can anything be more absurd than to impose a single style on the fat and the thin, on the minimum wage and the maximum income?

I admit that no fashion has ever been created expressly for the lean purse or for the fat woman: the dressmaker's ideal is undoubtedly the thin millionairess. But the fat woman and the lean purse must make the best of each style in turn, as it comes along. And if one has ever seen a fat woman in (for example) a hobble skirt—even in an academic edition of a hobble skirt—one knows that this is not a light thing to say. As for the lean purse, it is not only in alarmist articles that the working-girl goes without half her luncheons to buy a rhinestone sunburst. One has known the cases. Nor is the coercion purely psychological. The cheapest Eighth Avenue suit, which, ready-made, costs something-and-ninety-eight cents, is sure to be a hasty and sleazy imitation (at many removes, and losing something with each) of a Fifth Avenue model. It is one of the few true paradoxes that people who must dress cheaply must dress "in style." And that is a hard fate for the hypothetical poor woman with intelligence, who secretly desires a garment that will be no more conspicuous next year than this, and longs to put some of her money into good materials. It is only a very good (and expensive) dressmaker whose handiwork can both elude the exaggerations of the present fashion and foreshadow the essentials of the next. That is another thing that every woman knows.

The hypothetical poor woman with intelligence must content herself with looking a travesty on the successful chorus-girl. This, unfortunately, she comes only too easily to do. "But," some one might object, "the poor woman is precisely an economic, not an æsthetic consideration." Granted: yet since we must all dress, why not invent dresses that are widely adaptable—to different materials, to different occasions, to different human types? It would purge our streets of many a sorry and sordid spectacle, and in that sense would be an æsthetic service both particular and public. But, as it is, we must all dress alike: *blonde* and *brune,* fat and thin, tall and short, rich and poor. The socialists have threatened us with no more rigid sisterhood than this.

The principle of fashion is, as I have intimated, the principle of the kaleidoscope. A new year can only bring us a new combination of the same elements; and about once in so

often we go back and begin over. Recently we
have had rather a Napoleonic tendency. Occasionally we are Colonial. We have been known
to be Japanese. Now and then we have a
severe classic moment—usually very unbecom-
ing to all of us. We used to hear from our
grandmothers of silk dresses that could "stand
alone." What we need now is a silk dress that
could somehow manage to run.

There is no reward, in the world of
woman's dress, for a successful experiment.
The most charming design in the world has
no future. One is seldom tempted to apostro-
phize a fashion with, "Verweile doch! du bist so
schön!"; but if one were, the adjuration would
be as vain as ever. And that is another sin
against beauty, for it deprives a woman of the
privilege of dressing as best becomes her.
There is something peculiarly bitter in watching the superseding of a mode that wholly
suits one. Now and then a woman confides to
me her intention of keeping to some style that
is especially adapted to her. "It suits me, and
I am going to stick to it," she declares. She
has found that it makes the most of all her
"points"; it has given her, perhaps, renewed
respect for her appearance and fresh zest for
life. Such a woman is always, I believe, sincerely congratulated by her friends. They do
not imitate her, but they really and unmali-
ciously envy her her point of view. She is

proud of herself, and keeps to her decision for—say—a year. I never knew a woman to try such an experiment longer. She finds herself invariably conspicuous—and no well-bred woman likes to be unnecessarily conspicuous. For modesty's sake she must adopt the extravagance of the moment. Otherwise, she discovers herself to be not rational but "queer," and her attempt at wisdom to be the worst of affectations. It may be ironic that a woman who looks best in the mode of the Empress Josephine should be forced to dress *en chinoise;* but it is more than ironic when she has to dress *en chinoise* one year and *en grecque* the next. I have once or twice known elderly women who achieved something like a fixed costume for themselves; but they were semi-invalids. The consistent costume is, like the nun's habit, the best possible proof of having renounced the world.

And into what pits do the great *couturières* not fall in the search for something "new" enough to destroy the eligibility of all last year's frocks! I never knew what ladies patronized, a few years since, the London woman who invented "emotional dressmaking"; but I can testify to having seen, in a show-window of one of the largest department stores in America, a model from her—is not the word "atelier"? A large group of plain women were gathered, staring at it. I joined the group and read the legend. The name of the dress was "Passion's Thrall." At least, as the White Knight said, "that was what the name was *called.*" Within the shop, in the spirit of curiosity, I followed a similar group to the "department" where such things live. Again, the emotional dressmaker. Isolated in a glass drawing-room, stood two draped figures: "Her Dear Desire," and "Afterwards." I could have imagined some one's buying "Her Dear Desire"—it was of sad-colored chiffon. But I could not imagine any one's buying "Afterwards"; and it was inconceivable that the name should help to sell it. I am bound to say that eventually I found myself alone in the contemplation of this sartorial drama. The crowd had followed a living model who was illustrating the possibility and method of walking in the new "Paquin skirt." The gravity of every one concerned was unbelievable. Mr. Granville Barker has done some admirable satire on dressmaking in *The Madras House;* but his third act is positively less poignant than a reality like that.

Yet this is not the worst. Even if we said to ourselves, "Let us be always—but varyingly—ugly," we should not have phrased our greatest danger. Our greatest danger is simply the loss of all standards of beauty in dress. "Why do all the women walk like ducks this year?" was the question put to a friend of mine, years

[46]

since, by a younger brother. He did not know that a quite new kind of corset had suddenly, during the summer months, "come in." To wear it meant change of gait and posture, eventually actual change of shape. Yet we all wore it—and doubtless went on praising the Venus of Melos as we did so. The notion that, after we have learned from the scientists to deal in evolutionary periods of millions of years, we ought not naïvely to expect to alter the human form in a season or two, never occurred, I fancy, to any of us. "Business is business," men are credited with saying, when invited to apply abstract laws of honor. "Fashion is fashion," women would surely say if invited to apply abstract laws of beauty.

The worst thing is that the drapery or the trimming that is lovely and desirable in our eyes one year, is unspeakably offensive to our gaze the next. (Consider, for example, the chequered history of fringe!—its career like that of a French Pretender.) Fashion has vitiated our taste to that point. Our welcoming raptures are as sincere as our shuddering rejections. There was a time when sleeves could not—I say it advisedly—be too large. I remember seeing a girl turn to edge sideways through a large door, for fear of crushing the sleeves of a new bodice. Her brothers laughed; but I—I was very young—felt a pang of clear, unmitigated envy. I remember at that time prophecies that tight sleeves would never come in again—they were so ugly. Yet how many times, since then, have tight sleeves come in— and gone out? While, if one dared to make any prophecy about the clothes of the future, it would be that those *very* large sleeves would never again be worn: they are so hideous.

There is no point in pretending that one is superior to this fluctuating standard. One is not. Ideally speaking, every woman should keep the language of fashion and the language of taste rigidly apart. "Fashionable" and "beautiful" should not be used interchangeably. Theoretically, we all acknowledge the difference; but it is another matter when we are faced by the actual product. There may be, here and there, a woman who can say with sincerity, "She wore a hideous thing she has just got from Worth"; but where is the woman who could ingenuously report: "She had on a lovely frock made in the style of year before last"? I could not do it myself; nor, I fancy, could you. We may not like the new mode the very first time that we see it; we may pity before we endure; but we end by embracing. The bravest of us can do no more than criticize for its ugliness something fashionable. When it comes to praising for its beauty something unfashionable, the words stick in our throats. Clothes that are unfashionable simply do not look beautiful to us. Presently they may, when the kaleidoscope has been turned again; but not now. And that means that we have given up a good deal of intellectual freedom.

I have called the loss of æsthetic standards our greatest danger. One would prefer to think that it is. One likes to believe that the "prestige value" of the current mode is due to an honest if mistaken conviction of its beauty, not to the implications of income that both fashionable and unfashionable clothes make so definitely. It is pleasanter to say to one's self that the woman who refuses an invitation to dinner because her best frock is two years old fears criticism of her taste, than that she fears an estimate of her dressmaker's bill. The code is more alluring. But even assuming this to be the cause, the result is no less unfortunate: namely, an almost universal social timidity on the part of unfashionably dressed women—by which I mean, for the moment, nothing worse than women in frocks that were fashionable a season since. And that is a pity.

One does not, on the whole, regret history; and our institutions are by this time historic. I offer the suggestion as one who is glad, rather than sorry, that John Adams was not (according to his reputed desire) created Duke of Braintree. But an hereditary aristocracy serves some charming minor purposes, one of them being, perhaps, the social countenancing of dowdiness. A duchess may be as dowdy as she likes; and other women may with impunity be the less smart in a land where there are always duchesses being dowdy. I am sufficiently American, myself, not really to admire the typical Englishwoman's clothes. Half a dozen queer necklaces and a perfectly irrelevant bit of lace pinned on somewhere, do not atone to me for a faded straw hat at Christmas and a skirt that is six inches shorter in front than in back. Not many years ago, I went, with the briefest possible interval, from a British suffrage meeting to a dress-rehearsal at the Comédie Française. The resulting sensation amounted to a shock. "Frenchwomen could not dress like Englishwomen without conviction of sin," I said to my companion. "And ought not to," was his firm rejoinder. At the moment, I agreed with him. But there is something fine, after all, in the attitude of the woman who, having occasion to go to some "function" of a kind that she usually avoided, brought out a frock from her ten-year-old trousseau, and had it furbished up by a sempstress. The frock, I should say, had passed from her mother's trousseau into her own, having served for the former's presentation at court on the occasion of her marriage. It may be that an untitled woman could not have done it so debonairly. It would certainly be hard for a good American to follow her example. But the very idea

[50]

brings one such a hint of freedom as it takes—
they say—a limited monarchy to give.

Sensible people realize that children should
not be overdressed, and a few schools in this
country have adopted the conventual method
of putting their pupils into uniforms. But the
uniforms are, I fear, only another turn of the
kaleidoscope. I know that in one such school,
at least, the girls wear the school costume all
day, but dress in the evening as variously and
as elaborately as they choose. A rule like that
is *magnifique et pas cher*. For grown-ups, there
is no uniform at all. The fact is that we
are uncomfortable if we are not fashionably
dressed. No man understands the subtle and
complex significance of the phrase "nothing to
wear"—witness the distressed but utterly puz-
zled expression that overspreads a man's face
at the words. He knows that his wife or his
sister looks charming in "the blue one," or
"the lace one," or "the one with the jet." She
has looked charming in it often enough for
him at last to identify it—and that, unless he
is an exception to his sex, is very often. He is
cheerfully getting into his evening coat for the
fiftieth time. No wonder he does not realize
that some frock which, the first time it was
worn, made for triumph, should, the tenth
time, make for humiliation. But the most
strong-minded woman—the woman who will,
if necessary, go to the opera on a gala night in

a coat and skirt—at heart exonerates the woman who so foolishly, for the reason mentioned, stops at home.

There is much to be said, whether in the fifteenth century or the twentieth, for the aristocracy of wealth and all that it can do for the community in which it prevails. Neither Florence nor New York, probably, if consulted, would wish, or would have wished, to give up its Magnificent. But there are minor ways in which an aristocracy of wealth makes us all more sordid. Obviously, in these conditions, one's income must constitute one's claim to distinction, and, obviously, one can give mannerly evidence of one's income only by the amount visibly, not audibly, spent. How more silently and more visibly than by personal adornment? Is all this too trite to say? It behooves the man, for many reasons, not to adorn himself—perhaps, even, not in any merely personal way to outshine other men— while his wife may not only please herself but render his reputation a positive service by outshining other women. She makes no indiscreet disclosures of fact, but she rustles with pecuniary implications. In an aristocracy of wealth, Paris may go far to make a peeress of her.

I do not wish to imply that this is the sole American standard: there are communities in which "family" counts; and there are the academic backwaters where strange-scaled fish constitute among themselves aristocracies of intellect. It need hardly be said that in the latter places dress counts least of all. One may go to hear even the most distinguished lecturer in any rag one has; and we are judged rather by the obvious intention of a frock than by its actual achievement. There is so much of Oxford in any of our college towns. But no one can deny that the aristocracy most widely developed in America is that of wealth. It is developed in places that are really too small to afford an aristocracy at all. I myself have known women whose fathers carried dinner-pails and whose husbands have never even stopped to regret that their own education ended with the grammar-school course, who simply did not feel that the shabbily or simply dressed woman could be in their class. She may be descended from a half a dozen Signers, and be at home in every picture-gallery in Europe, but she is some one to whom, socially, they cannot but condescend.

I am told that precisely the same standards prevail in the newer urban civilizations of England: it would seem to be an inevitable immediate result of the supremacy of riches. There is perhaps no limit to the sophistication that vast wealth can eventually give to its own possessors; but this law of fashion is what, consciously or unconsciously, they impose on the seething estates beneath them. I have known

tragedies in smallish American cities that began and ended in dress: women deprived of
their all too infrequent intellectual and social
delights, simply because they could not bring
themselves to face an assembly in which other
women whose authority their own taste could
not acknowledge, knew their "best" dresses by
heart.

I have said that the economic considerations
are no concern of mine; nor are they. Yet it
may not be amiss to suggest in this context
that the women who are responsible for the
almost unpaid toil of the slum-children over
"willow" plumes are not the rich women who
will give for their willow plumes any price that
is asked of them. It is the harpy of the sub-
urbs, the frequenter of bargain-counters and
Monday morning "sales," the woman whose
most instructive reading is done among the
designs and patterns of the "women's" magazines, who is responsible. From what one
reads, one is certainly compelled to infer that
if these little children are to be saved, willow
plumes should be put at prohibitive prices.
"But since our women *must* walk gay," the
aristocracy that is rooted in democracy can
hardly do without its willow plumes. Fashion
has got itself into a position of such importance as that. It is so terrible a thing to be
unfashionable that the vast majority of women
—and the vast majority of women are not rich

or anything like it—stretch every nerve to be
in fashion. They miss, if they are not, too
much that is legitimately theirs. The require-
ment is irrelevant, is absurd; but it is made.
They will, therefore, pay what they can; but
they cannot pay much. The logic is clear. They
go to the great shops to demand their willow
plumes, and their Irish-lace collars, in the very
spirit which took the Dames de la Halle to
Versailles. Hence many of the conditions of
labor about which we read so many lurid
articles. For demand creates supply.

The American woman of moderate income
is alternately congratulated on her "smartness"
and scolded for her extravagance. She cannot
very well, as things stand, be smart without
being extravagant. But the fact that chiefly
gives one pause is this: that a woman cannot
mingle comfortably with her equals unless she
can clothe herself each season in a way that
both to her and to them would have looked
preposterous a twelvemonth before. It has
luckily become, in the strictest sense, vulgar, to
be *endimanchée;* but most people are—by definition—vulgar; and I have known women,
again, who stayed at home from church because they could not so clothe themselves. Not
unadvisedly, I am tempted to say; for in one
of the most famous churches of America, I
have seen the shabbily dressed woman seated,
by the usher, with reference solely to her cos-

tume; and I have heard, too, the testimony of other women of her kind, turned into "stay-at-homes" because precisely that thing they could not endure. An odd battle of pride with pride; and there are better uses to put pride to than that. More blatant and less grim is the authentic anecdote recently told me concerning a Newport "colonist." She and her daughter entered the church one Sunday morning, marvellously dressed in contrasting shades of red. "There will be no one else in our pew this morning," she murmured graciously to the usher; "put some one in with us, if you like— any one in white or black." What could not Dean Swift have done with that! One does not wish to make tragedy out of what is essentially comic. Yet it may fairly be said that comedy has its rough side, and that a comedy retold from the point of view of the comic character himself, would often make melancholy stuff. It would be possible, over this matter of fashion, to shed the bitter tears of the satirist.

It is odd that "dress reform" should always have meant something ugly. There would be so tremendous a chance for any one who wished to reform dress in the interest of beauty! But the most amused and disgusted of us will, very likely, forever shrink from the task. "The pilgrims were clothed with such kind of raiment as was diverse from the raiment of any that traded in that fair. The people, therefore, of the fair made a great gazing upon them: some said they were fools, some they were bedlams, and some they were outlandish men." There are two reasons why we shall shrink from it: we should have to begin with ourselves; and we should certainly be called bedlams. But oh, the pity of it!

CAVIARE ON PRINCIPLE

ONE can usually either begin or end with Mr. Chesterton, though one can seldom do both. "It is simpler to eat caviare on impulse than to eat grape-nuts on principle," he says, in one of his intervals of pure lucidity. I should like to make a Chestertonian transposition, and pronounce that it is better (I do not say simpler) to eat caviare on principle than to eat grape-nuts on impulse. The fact is that the modern fad of simplicity for its own sake has ceased to be merely ridiculous; it has become dangerous. May not some of us lift our voices against it?

I have no right, I suppose, to ally, in my own mind, socialists and vegetarians. But I nearly always find, when I ask a vegetarian if he is a socialist, or a socialist if he is a vegetarian, that the answer is in the affirmative. I am sure that they, on their side, confuse snobs with meat-eaters. One could forgive them, were they more bitterly logical. For my own part, I should be quite willing to go the length of all Hinduism and say that rice itself has a soul. I can even see myself joining a "movement" for giving the vote to violets and disfranchising orchids. This, however, is not their desire. They do not wish to make even the ox a citizen—only a brother; and I have never discovered that vegetarians—even when they were "hygienic," not "sentimental," ones— were anxious to reproduce the history of the rice-fed peoples. But let their logic take care of itself. My point is really that socialists and vegetarians are banded together to fight for the simplifying of life. Socialism, of course, organizes as furiously as Capital itself; and I leave it to any one if a nut-cutlet is not complicated to the point of mendacity. But ostensibly both sects are on the side of Procrustes against human vagaries. Both would surely consider caviare immoral; either because no one ought to eat it, or because every one cannot. It does not much matter, I fancy, which point you make against the dried roe of the sturgeon. My own plea for caviare rests precisely on the fact that it is not, and cannot be, thrust into every one's mouth. It is not simple, no. The only really "simple" food-stuff is manna. Imagine, for example, calling anything simple that has to be shot out of a cannon by way of preparation. In point of fact, very few people eat caviare save on impulse,—otherwise, they find it too nasty. But it is an impulse worthy of being dogmatized; of becoming a principle.

Simplicity is an acquired taste. Mankind, left free, instinctively complicates life. The hardest command to follow has always been

[59]

that which bids us take no thought for the morrow. Perhaps that is what Mr. Chesterton means when he talks of the difficulty of eating grape-nuts on principle. The real drawback to "the simple life" is that it is not simple. If you are living it, you positively can do nothing else. There is not time. For the simple life demands virtually that there shall be no specialization. The *Hausfrau* who is living the simple life must, after all, sweep, scour, wash, and mend. She must also cook; from that, even Battle Creek cannot save her. She may dream sternly of Margaret Fuller, who read Plato while she pared apples; but in her secret heart she knows that either Plato or the apples suffered. And from what point of view is it simpler to have a maid-of-all-work than to indulge one's self in liveried lackeys? Not, obviously, for the mistress; and it is surely simpler to be an adequate second footman than to be an adequate *bonne-à-tout-faire*. We should really simplify life by having more servants rather than fewer; more luxury instead of less. The smoothest machinery is the most complicated; and which of us wants to sink the Mauretania and go back to Robert Fulton's steamboat? One would think that the decision would be made naturally for one by one's income. But it is the triumph of the new paradox that this is not so. Thousands of people seem to be infected with the idea that by doing more themselves they bestow leisure on others; that by wearing shabby clothes they somehow make it possible for others to dress better—though they thus admit tacitly that leisure and elegance are not evil things. Or perhaps—though Heaven forbid they should be right!—they merely think that by refusing nightingales' tongues, they make every one more content with porridge. Let us be gallant about the porridge that we must eat, but let us never forget that there are better things to eat than porridge.

> And all time past, was it all for this?
> Times unforgotten, and treasures of things?

What is the use of throwing great museums open to the people, if you tell them at the same time that to possess the contents of the museums would not make a private person happier? Why should there be *cordons bleus* in the world, if we ought to live on bread and milk? Above all, why have we praised, through the centuries, all the slow processes, the tardy consummations, of perfection, if raw material, either in art or life, is really best? I recall at this instant a friend of mine who expresses her democracy in her footwear. Her frocks are as charming as money can induce Paquin to make them; but if her frocks are an insult to the poor, her boots are an insult to the rich. I have seen her walk to a garden-party, in real lace, and out at heel. She fancied, I think, that her inadequate boots obliterated the deplorable social distinction between herself and her cook. In point of fact, her cook would not have condescended to them; would not have considered herself a "lady" if she had.

I have other friends who feel strongly the ignominy of personal service: who agree with many ignorant young women that it is more dignified to be a bullied, insulted, underpaid shop-girl with a rhinestone sunburst, than a well-paid, highly-respected parlor-maid in a uniform. Accordingly, they conscientiously deprive themselves of the parlor-maid, and spend her wages in trying to get a vote for the shop-girl. I do not understand their distinctions in liberty, or their definition of degradation. The parlor-maid at least can choose the mistress, but the shop-girl cannot choose the floor-walker.

I am, myself, essentially an undomestic woman, and I dislike the parlor-maid's tasks to the point of feeling excessive irritation at having, occasionally, in this mad world, to perform them. But, seriously speaking, apart from the temperamental quirk, I would don her clothes and follow officially her career, rather than that parlor-maids in uniforms should pass wholly from the world. It is as if these people said, "Since those who are parlor-maids themselves cannot very well employ parlor-maids, then let no one have a parlor-maid." Their factitious altruism, with all its peril, might be forgiven them; but the misguided creatures (who are human beings and egotists, after all, and as such must "save their face") go on to say that it is really much nicer not to have parlor-maids. And that lie is unpardonable, for it strikes at the root of human experience. Parlor-maids would never have become a convention if they had not been found desirable.

Are we really, at this late day, going to be duped by the mid-century fallacy that "plain living and high thinking" are a natural combination? Even if Shakespeare at New Place teaches us nothing, we cannot fail to be impressed by the memory of Thoreau, stealing home from Lake Walden by dark, to provide himself secretly with better fare than the woods afforded. As if, indeed, any one who had tried plain living did not know that high thinking was done, if at all, in spite of it! "The hand of little employment hath the daintier sense," as Shakespeare long since said. Let us open our own front doors, polish our own shoes, dust our own bibelots, and make messes on a chafing-dish when the cook is out; and let us do it gallantly. But let us not pretend that it is more civilized to do these things ourselves than to have them skilfully done for us. The prince in disguise makes the most charming beggar in the world, no doubt; but that is because—as all fairy-tales from the beginning of time have taught us—the prince wears his rags as if they were purple. And, to do that, he not only must once have worn purple, but must never forget the purple that he has worn. And to the argument that all cannot wear purple, I can, as I say, only reply that that seems to me to be no reason why all should wear rags.

Until every one is too good to be a parlor-maid, let us open our own doors, if we must—provided we do it according to the great tradition of door-opening; but how can we do it according to the great tradition if we abolish parlor-maids and dry up the fount of the great tradition? And, whatever the simplifiers say, there is no doubt that, as yet, there are, to one person who is too good for door-opening, ten persons who are by no means good enough for it. I have never been able to imagine just how the sound of the Last Trump is going to shiver the aristocracy of earth into the democracy of Heaven. To be sure, it is not my affair. But at least one can have, this side the grave, little patience with the altruisms of the Procrusteans. They merely wish to make each of us an incompetent Jack-at-all-trades. And one had thought the German universities, if they had done nothing else, had blown that bubble!

A friend of mine asked me the other day if I did not feel degraded to be at the mercy of servants; humiliated by knowing that they could perform domestic tasks better than I, and could take advantage of that fact. I confess it had never occurred to me. If my cook felt degraded by being unable to talk French, I should think her a silly snob. Are we not all, economically, at one another's mercy? Of what does enthusiastic living of the "simple" life make us independent, save of a few hard-learned and precious lessons of taste? The successful housewife is the one who has succeeded in imitating perfectly several trained servants. But the criterion is still the trained servant. The distinguished beggar is the one who wears his rags as if they were purple. But, to appreciate him, we must know the look of purple rightly worn. The admirable vegetarian eats his shredded wheat as if it were caviare. But where would be the beauty of his performance were not someone, somewhere, eating caviare as if it were shredded wheat?

THE EXTIRPATION OF CULTURE

IT is odd how words recur. There has been more talk about culture, among educated people in America, during the last months, than there had been for years. To be sure, the culture discussed since August, 1914, has been German Kultur; but that does not matter. We have actually been talking about culture once more; rehabilitating it, if only for the sake of denying that the Germans, by and large, have a monopoly of anything so good. To some of us, this recurrence of a word so long *tabu* is welcome—and as side-splittingly funny as it is welcome. For the fact is that for twenty years —ever since Matthew Arnold went out of fashion—to speak of culture has meant that one did not have it. The only people who have talked about it have been the people who have thought you could get it at Chautauquas. To use the word damned you in the eyes of the knowing. Now I have always, privately and humbly, thought it a pity that so good a word should go out of the best vocabularies; for when you lose an abstract term, you are very apt to lose the thing it stands for. Indeed, it has seemed only too clear that we were doing all in our power to lose both the word and the thing. I fancy we ought to be grateful to the Germans for getting "culture" on to all the editorial pages of the country; though I admit it sometimes seems as if the Germans bore out the rule that only those people talk about it who have it not. I should really like to make a plea for the temporary reversal of the rule. Indeed, I think we are getting to a point where we are so little "cultured" that we can really afford to talk about it. When the plutocrat goes bankrupt, he may once more, with decency, mention the prices of things. Culture has ceased to be a passionate American preoccupation. Perhaps we shall not offend modesty if we use the word once more.

Now there are some who, believing that all is for the best in the best of possible worlds, and that to-morrow is necessarily better than to-day, may think that if culture is a good thing we shall infallibly be found to have more of it than we had a generation since; and that if we can be shown not to have more of it, it can be shown not to be worth seeking. Having, myself, a congenital case of agoraphobia, I habitually say nothing to the professional optimists in the public square. The wilderness is a good place to cry in; the echoes are magnificent. So I shall not attempt to deprive any one of Candide's happy conviction. If any person is kind enough to listen, I will simply ask him to contemplate a few facts with me.

[67]

No one will be too optimistic, I fancy, to grant that there are *proportionally* fewer Americans who care about culture—and who know the real thing when they see it—than there were one or two generations ago. Contact with "the best that has been thought and said in the world" is not desired by so large a proportion of the community as it was. That there are new and *parvenu* branches of learning, furiously followed, I, on my part, shall not attempt to deny. But culture is another matter. Perhaps the sociologists can show that this is a good thing. I do not ask any one to deplore anything. I only ask the well-disposed to examine the change that has come over the spirit of our American dream.

If I were asked to give, off hand, the causes of the gradual extirpation of culture among us, I should name the following:

1. The increased hold of the democratic fallacy on the public mind.

2. The influx of a racially and socially inferior population.

3. Materialism in all classes.

4. The idolatry of science.

Only one of these is purely intellectual; two might almost be called political. In point of fact, all four are interwoven.

I should be insultingly trite if I proceeded here to expound the fallacy of the historic statement that all men are born free and equal.

We have all known for a long time that individual freedom and individual equality cannot co-exist. I dare say no one since Thomas Jefferson (and may I express my doubts even of that inspired charlatan?) has really believed it. No one could believe it at the present day except the people who are flattered by it; and of people who are flattered by it, it is obviously not true. The democracy of the present day—like the aristocracy of another day—is fostered by the people whom it advantages; and the people whom it advantages are adding themselves, at the rate of a million a year, to our census lists. When even democracy has to reckon with the fact that its premises are all wrong, and that men are not born equal—that hierarchies are inherent in human kind regardless of birth or opportunity—it proceeds to do its utmost to equalize artificially; it becomes Procrustes. But will any one contend that Procrustes left people free?

Now, what has this to do with culture? Simply this: that culture is not a democratic achievement, because culture is inherently snobbish. Contact with "the best that has been thought and said in the world" makes people intellectually exclusive, and makes them draw distinctions. Those distinctions, seriously speaking, are not founded on social origins or great possessions; they are founded on states of mind. So long as democracy is simply a political matter, culture is left free to select its groups and proclaim its hierarchies. But it is characteristic of our democracy that political equality has not sufficed to it; the "I am as good as you are" formula has been flung out to every horizon. The people with whom it has become a mania insist that their equality with every one else in their range of vision is a moral, an intellectual, a social, as well as a political, equality. Let that formula prevail, and culture, with its eternal distinction-drawing, will naturally die. For contact with the best that has been thought and said in the world induces a mighty humility —and a mighty scorn of those who do not know enough to be humble before the Masters. They are an impersonal humility and an impersonal scorn—attitudes of the mind, both, not of the heart. But humility and scorn are both ruled, theoretically, out of the democratic court.

The pure-bred American once cared for culture, and no longer—to the same extent, at least—does. If any one asks why America (I use the word loosely, as meaning our United States), having always, since the Revolution, been a democracy, can have cared for so undemocratic a thing, the answer is simple. The democracy of our forefathers was a purely pragmatic affair. The Declaration of Independence was framed by men living in a world where it was almost true enough to be workable. Roughly speaking, in pioneer and colonial days—wherever and whoever the pioneers and colonists may be—the community is a democracy because it is an aristocracy. In those grimmer worlds, the fittest do survive because there is no incubator process to keep the feeble going. A pioneer and colonial group, moreover, is apt to be like-minded; people do not exile themselves in each other's company unless they want the same things. Minor differences of opinion are swallowed up in like major needs: you form coalition governments against savages and famine or a specially detested tyranny. In the modern "I am as good as you are" sense, our ancestors were not democratic at all. They were democratic for their own special group, and a pragmatic truth misled them—as, because we admire them, we are permitting it to mislead us. They were Brahminical in their attitude to learning; they thought it supremely valuable, and they did not believe in—no Brahmin wants to believe in—a royal road to it, any more than they believed in a royal road to the salvation of the soul. They believed in intellectual, as much as they did in spiritual, election; and they certainly did not think that politics could influence either. Up to the last generation or two, they looked upon the cultured man as a peculiarly favored person; and because culture (unlike beauty, let us say) depended to some extent on the effort of the individual, they thought it fit to mention.

Now there is this about a pragmatic truth:

like any other invention of the devil, it
smooths the road for the lazy. If it did not
smooth the road, it would not be, by pragmatic
definition, truth. And the great bulk of us have
found the "free and equal" statement such a
help that, though we cannot pretend for a
moment that it is true, we stick to it. The
schoolboy sticks to it because it greases his
oratory; the politician sticks to it because his
constituents like the sound of it; the detrimen-
tal sticks to it because it is his only apology.
And, just as you cannot suppress a word without eventually suppressing the thing it stands
for, so you cannot utter a statement forever
without imbibing some of its poison. Even as
our reasonable national pride turned into the
spread-eagleism that Dickens and Mrs. Trol-
lope caricatured, so the "free and equal" shib-
boleth turned into the "I am as good as you
are" formula. Why trouble about anything, if
you were already lord of the world? At first,
it was Europe we defied. What were the ancient oligarchies, to impose on us their standards, intellectual, social, or moral? We set
up our own standards, because we were as
good as any one else—and also because it was
a little easier.

Let me say before going further, that I am
not blaming the lower classes alone for the
extirpation of culture among us. The upper
classes are equally responsible—if, indeed, not

even more to blame. We have become materialistic: our very virtues are more materialistic than they were. It is forgivable in the poor man to be materialistic; for unless he has bread to keep his body alive, he will presently have no soul to cherish. Materialism is less pardonable in the man who always knows where his next meal is coming from. He, if you like, does have time to worry about his soul. None the less, he worries about it very little. There used to be a good deal of fun poked at settlement-workers who tried to read Dante and Shakespeare to slum-dwellers. I am not sure that those misguided youths and maidens who first carried Dante and Shakespeare into the slums were not right as to substance, however wrong they were as to sequence. The only morally decent excuse for wanting to have a little more money than you actually need to feed and clothe your family, is your ambition to have a little mental energy to spend on things not of the body. The ultimate tragedy of the slums is that, in slum conditions, one can scarcely think, from birth to death, of anything but the body. The upper-class people who think of pleasing their palates instead of relieving hunger, of being in the fashion instead of covering their nakedness, are no more civilized than the slum-dwellers. They are apt, it is true, to become more so; for it is a strange fact that a family can seldom be rich through several generations without discovering some æsthetic truths. And æsthetic truths lead to moral perceptions. You cannot with impunity fill your ears with good music, your eyes with good painting and sculpture and architecture. Something happens to you, after a time, no matter how vulgar you may be. But wealth is very fluctuating in our country; and several generations of it are not often seen. The people who are now rich are generally people whose grandfathers and great-grandfathers were fighting for sheer existence. So we have the spectacle of the dominant plutocrats (no one will deny that plutocracy is the order of the day, both here and in Europe) either mindful themselves of the struggle for existence, or in a state of having only just forgotten it. They are not going to push their children into a race for intangible goods. And the more we recruit from immigrants who bring no personal traditions with them, the more America is going to ignore the things of the spirit. No one whose consuming desire is either for food or for motor-cars is going to care about culture, or even know what it is. And it is another misfortune of our over-quickened social evolution that the middle classes do not stay middle-class. They climb to wealth, or sink to indigence. Neither that quick rise nor that quick fall is a period in which to cherish their own or their children's intellects.

Both from above and below, then, our colleges and schools have felt the hostile pressure. Colleges are, on the one hand, jeered at for doing their business badly, and, on the other, accused of being too difficult. We are always hearing that college is of no earthly use to a man except as he learns there to rub up against other men. We are always hearing, also, that the college curriculum is a cruel strain on the average boy or girl. On one score or another, the colleges are always being attacked; and the attack usually includes the hint that the real test of a "college education" is not the intrinsic value, but its success or failure in preparing the youth for something that has nothing to do with learning. Will it be of social or financial use to him? If not, why make sacrifices to get it? Far be it from me to assert that the intellectual flame never burns in the breast of collegiate youth! But I do believe it provable that there is far less tendency to regard learning as a good in itself, and far more tendency to cheat scholarship, if possible, in the interest of some other thing held good, than there was two generations ago. Ignorance of what real learning is, and a consequent suspicion of it; materialism, and a consequent intellectual laxity—both of these have done destructive work in the colleges.

The education of younger children is in like case. We put them into kindergartens where their reasoning powers are ruined; or, if we can afford it, we buy Montessori outfits that were invented for semi-imbeciles in Italian slums; or we send them to outdoor schools and give them prizes for sleeping. Every one knows what a fight the old universities have had to put up to keep their entrance standards at all. With the great new army of state universities admitting students from the public schools without examination, because they themselves are part of the big public-school system, how can it be otherwise?

Now the patriotic American may see—and rightly enough—in the public-school system which includes a college training, a relic of the desperate desire of our forefathers that education, as a major good, should be within the reach of all and sundry. But even the patriotic American must see another impulse at work: the impulse to put the college intellectually, as well as financially, within the reach of all. The colleges must not set up standards for themselves that the average boy or girl, from the ordinary school, cannot reach without difficulty, because that is undemocratic.

Now I know as well as other people that it is positively harder to get into our old universities to-day than it was in our fathers' day. But granted the enormously increased facilities for preparation all over the land, it is not relatively anything like so hard. Certainly, once in, it is possible to get through the college course with less work than ever before. In the first place, there is a much wider choice of subjects on which a boy can get his degree: his tastes are consulted as they never used to be. If he does not want to endure the discipline of Greek, he can get an A.B. at every college in the country—except Princeton—without knowing a word of Greek. Even at Princeton, he can take a Litt.B. and let Greek forever alone.* He can study sociology, or Spanish, or physical culture, or nearly anything he likes. I have even heard that in one of our state universities there is a department of hat-trimming, which contributes its quota to the courses for a (presumably feminine) academic degree.

It may be objected at this point that the fluctuations of colleges have nothing to do with our standards of culture. I think they have, a great deal. No one will deny that culture can be got elsewhere, or that colleges do not suffice in themselves to give it. But if colleges do not consider themselves custodians of culture, warders and cherishers of the flame, they have no reason for existence. It is a platitude that

* I have been told, since writing this essay, that the University of Chicago demands a modicum of Greek for the A. B. degree. The Catholic University does the same. And it is only fair to say, also, that, since this essay was written, Princeton has abdicated her well-nigh unique position. It will hereafter be possible to acquire the Princeton A. B. without knowing *alpha* from *omega*.

business men consider college a worthless preparation for business life—save as a young man may have laid up there treasure for himself in the shape of valuable "connections." Even the conception of college as a four years' paradise intervening before the hell of an active struggle for existence, does not touch upon the original reason for universities' being at all. Universities were invented for the sake of bringing their fortunate students into contact with the precious lore of the world, there garnered and kept pure. There was no idea on the part of their founders that every one would or could partake of academic benefits. The social scheme would not originally have allowed that; still less would the conception of the public intellect have admitted the notion. Every one was not supposed to be congenitally qualified for intimacy with the best that has been thought and said in the world. They had no notion, until very recently, of so changing the terms of that intimacy that every one might think he could have it. Learning, culture, were not to be adulterated so that any mental digestive process whatsoever could take them in.

But now, in America, there is a tendency that way. If a boy does not feel a pre-established harmony between his soul and the humanities, then give him an academic degree on something with which his soul will be in pre-

established harmony. And if there is no pre-
established harmony between his soul and any
form of learning, then create institutions that
will give him a degree with no learning to
speak of at all. I do not mean to deny that
many of our virtually valueless colleges were
founded in the pathetic inherited conviction
that learning and culture were too great goods
not to be accessible to all who cared passionately for them. But I do believe that the reverence for learning and culture has been largely
replaced by a conviction that anything which
has so great a reputation as a college degree
must be put within the reach of all, even at the
risk of making its reputation a farce. The
privileged have been unwilling that their children should be made to work; the unprivileged
have been unwilling that their children should
see anything of good repute, anything with a
prestige value, denied to them. We have all
demanded a royal road to a thing to which
there is no royal road. The expensive schools
lead their pupils from kindergarten to nature-
study and eurhythmics, with basket-work and
gymnastics thrown in; the public schools follow
them as closely as they can. Of real training of
the mind there is very little in any school. The
rich do not want their children overworked;
the poor want a practical result for their
children's fantastically long school hours. So
domestic science comes in for girls, and car-

pentering for boys. Anything to make it easy, on the one hand; anything to make a universal standard possible, on the other.

Take one example only: the attitude towards Greek. There are two arguments against teaching our children Greek: one, that it is too hard; the other, that it is useless. The mere fact that public opinion has drummed Greek out of court as an inevitable part of a college curriculum shows that these arguments have been potent. No person who could be influenced by either has the remotest conception of the meaning or the value of culture. Culture has never renounced a thing because it was difficult, or because it did not help people to make money. And the mere fact that Greek is no longer supposed by the vast majority of parents to be of any "use"—even as a matter of reputation—to their sons, shows that the old standards of culture have changed. The larger number of our public schools no longer teach Greek at all; a great many private schools have to make special arrangements for pupils who wish to study it. And the attitude towards Greek is only a sign of our democratic, materialistic times.

Now I have done with the colleges. I have dealt with them at all only by way of hinting that they have been so democratized that culture means, even to its avowed exponents, something different from what it has ever meant before. May I speak for one moment explicitly of the public schools? For we must trace all this back to the source—must begin with the ostensible homes of "culture" and follow up the stream to the latent public consciousness. Each class that comes into college has read fewer and fewer of what are called the classics of English literature. An astonishing number of boys and girls have read nothing worth reading except the books that are in the entrance requirements. An increasing proportion of the sons and daughters of the prosperous are positively illiterate at college age. They cannot spell; they cannot express themselves grammatically; and they are inclined to think that it does not matter. General laxity, and the adoption of educational fads which play havoc with real education, are largely responsible. In the less fortunate classes, the fact seems to be that the public schools are so swamped by foreigners that all the teachers can manage to do is to teach the pupils a little workable English. Needless to say, the profession of the public-school teacher has become less and less tempting to people who are really fit for it.

It is not only in the great cities that the immigrant population swamps the schoolroom. An educated woman told me, not long since, that there was no school in the place where she lived—one of our oldest New England towns—to which she could send her boy. The town could not support a private school for young children; and the public school was out of the question. I had been brought up to believe that public schools in old New England towns were very decent places; and I asked her why. The answer made it clear. Three fourths of the school-children were Lithuanians, and a decently bred American child could simply learn nothing in their classes. They had to be taught English, first of all; they approached even the most elementary subjects very slowly; and — natural corollary — the teachers themselves were virtually illiterate. Therefore she was teaching her boy at home until he could go to a preparatory school. Fortunately, she was capable of doing it; but there are many mothers who cannot ground their children in the languages and sciences. A woman who could not would have had to watch her child acquiring a Lithuanian accent and the locutions of the slum.

An isolated case is never worth much. But one has only to consider conditions at large to see that this has everything to make it typical. One has only to look at any official record of immigration, any chart of distribution of population by races, to see how the old American stock is being numerically submerged. If you do not wish to look at anything so dull as statistics, look at the comic papers. A fact

does not become a stock joke until it is pretty
well visible to the average man. Our forefathers cared immensely for education; they
felt themselves humble before learning; and
their schools followed, soon and sacredly, upon
their churches. They stood in awe of the real
thing; and they had no illusions as to the ease
of the scholar's path. They legislated for their
schools solemnly, and if not with complete
wisdom, always at least with accurate ideals.
Educational (like all other) legislation nowadays is largely in the hands of illiterate
people, and the illiterate will take good care
that their illiteracy is not made a reproach to
them. If any one chooses to say that culture
must always be in the hands of an oligarchy,
and that the oligarchy has not been touched,
I will only ask him to consider the pupils and
the teaching in most private schools. In the
end, prestige values are going to tell; and the
vast bulk of our population will see to it that
the prestige values are not absolutely unattainable to them. The great fortunes have made
their way to the top—yes, really to the top. In
many cases there has been time for a quick
veneer of grammar to be laid over their original English. In many cases there has not; and
no one cares. The custodians of culture cannot
afford to care; for their custody must either
be endowed or be forsaken.

Oh, yes, there are a few Brahmins left; but

one has only to look at the marriages of any given season to see what is becoming of the purity of the Brahmin caste. The Brahmins themselves are beginning to see that they are lost unless they compound with the materialists, and make or marry money—or increase, by aid of the materialists, what they have inherited. In what New England village, now, is the minister or the scholar looked up to as a fount of municipal wisdom because he is a learned man? Is he a "good mixer"? That is what they ask: I have heard them. Once it was possible in America for a poor man to hope to gain for his children, if they deserved it, the life of the intellect and of the spirit. Now it no longer is; for the poor themselves have defiled the fount. They are a different kind of poor, that is all; and they have become an active and discontented majority, with hands that pick and steal. When they no longer need to pick and steal, they carry their infection higher and give it as a free gift. And they have been aided by the Brahmins themselves; who, having dabbled in sociology *pour se désoeuvrer*, and then for charity's sake, are now finding that sociology is a grim matter of life and death, and endow chairs of it—as if one should endow chairs of self-preservation. But self-preservation is not culture and never will be; and no study of the manners and customs of savages or slums can call itself "contact with the best that has been thought and said in the world."

We owe, too, I think, a great deal of our cultural deterioration (which I admit is a villainous phrase) to science. Science has come in with a rush, and is at present—why deny it?—on top. "Scientific" is a word to charm with, even though it has already had time to be degraded. If Mrs. Eddy had called her bargain-counter Orientalism anything but "science," would she have drawn so many followers? Science has done great things for us; it has also pushed us hopelessly back. For, not content with filling its own place, it has tried to supersede everything else. It has challenged the super-eminence of religion; it has turned all philosophy out of doors except that which clings to its skirts; it has thrown contempt on all learning that does not depend on it; and it has bribed the skeptics by giving us immense material comforts. To the plea, "Man shall not live by bread alone, but by every word which proceedeth out of the mouth of God," it has retorted that no word proceeds authentically out of the mouth of God save what it has issued in its own translations. It is more rigorous and more exclusive than the Index of the Roman Church. The Inquisition never did anything so oppressive as to put all men, innocent or guilty, into a laboratory. Science cares supremely for physical things. If it restricted itself to the physical world, it would be tolerable: we could shut ourselves away with our souls in peace. But it must control the soul as

well as the body: it insists on reducing all emotions, however miraculous and dear, to a question of nerve-centres. There has never been
tyranny like this.

Now I do not mean to say that all scientists
despise culture. That would be silly and untrue.
But the "scientific" obsession has changed all
rankings in the intellectual world. The insidi-
ousness of science lies in its claim to be not a
subject, but a method. You could ignore a subject: no subject is all-inclusive. But a method
can plausibly be applied to anything within the
field of consciousness. Small wonder that the
study of literature turns into philology, the
study of history into archæology, and the study
of morals and æsthetics into physical psychology. With the finer appeals of philosophy and
poetry and painting and natural beauty, science
need not meddle; because about their direct
effect on the thought and wills of men it can
say nothing valuable. You cannot determine
the value of a Velasquez by putting your finger
on the pulse of the man who is looking at it;
or the value of Amiens Cathedral by register-
ing the vibration of his internal muscles; or of
the Grand Cañon of the Colorado by declaring
that all perception of beauty is a function of
sex. Nor does it matter very much, at the
moment, to the enraptured reader or observer
that such and such a work of art was the
logical result of a given set of conditions. The

[86]

point is that it is there; and that it works potently upon us in ways which we can scarce phrase. Culture puts us disinterestedly in communication with the distilled and sifted lore of the world. Science is in comparison a prejudiced affair—prejudiced because it seeks always to bring things back to literal and physical explanations. Far be it from me to deny that geology, biology, physics, have given us unapprehended vistas down which to stray— only, strictly speaking, it forbids the straying. The moment the layman's imagination begins to profit, begins to get real exhilaration from scientific discoveries, it contributes something unwelcome to science. Science has its own stern value; in the end we are all profoundly affected by its gains in the field of fact. One's quarrel is not with science as such, but with science as demanding an intellectual and spiritual hegemony. With nothing less than hegemony, however, will science be content.

Now if it is not yet clear what effect all this must have on culture, a few words may make it clearer. The great danger of the scientific obsession is not the destruction of all things that are not science, but the slow infection of those things. If the laboratory is your real test, then most philosophies and all art are no good. The scientists are not good philosophers, and they are not good artists; and if science is to rule everywhere, we must shelve philosophy

and art, or else take them into the laboratory.
I need not point out what has become of literature under a scientific régime. We all know
the hopeless fiction that is created by the scientific method; fiction that banks on its anec-
dotal accuracy and has in it no spiritual truth.
Literature is simply a different game: you do
not get the greatest literary truth by the laboratory method. Art is not reducible to science,
because science takes no account of the special
truth which is beauty, of the special truth which
is moral imagination.

It is not only by the laboratory method that
our fiction has been ruined: a great many of
our writers of fiction are not up to the laboratory method. But all our fiction has been
harmed by the prevalent idea that no fiction is
any good which is not done according to the
laboratory method, and that even fiction which
attempts that method is of little value in comparison with a card-catalogue. There were some
snobs who were not affected by the democratic
fallacy; but even the snobs have been affected
by scientific scorn.

I may have seemed to be showing rather the
reasons for the extirpation of culture among us
than the fact of the extirpation. Perhaps that
is not the best way to go to work. But the
actual evidence is so multitudinously at hand
that it was hardly worth while beginning with
solemn proofs of the fact. In all branches of

art and learning we have a cult of the modern. Modern languages rank Latin and Greek in our schools and colleges; practical and "vocational" training is displacing the rudiments of learning in all of our public and many of our private institutions for the teaching of the young; the books admitted to the lists of "literature" include many that never have been and never will be literature. I found, a few years ago, the following books on a list from which students of English were allowed to choose their reading for the course—this, in one of the old and respectable high schools of Massachusetts, not twenty miles from Boston: *Soldiers of Fortune, Pushing to the Front, Greifenstein, Doctor Latimer, The Prisoner of Zenda, The Honorable Peter Stirling, The First Violin,* and "any of the works of Stewart Edward White." These, and many others, may be, in their way, good reading, but there is no excuse for offering them to the young student of English as examples of "literature."

Standards of beauty and truth are no longer rigidly held up. In philosophy we have produced pragmatism; in art we have produced futurism —and what not, since then?—in literature we have produced the pathologic and the economic novel, and no poetry worth speaking of. The "grand style" has gone out; and the classics are back numbers. Our children do not even speak good English; and no one minds. They

cannot be bored with Scott and Dickens; they
cannot be bored with poetry at all. And why
should they, when their fathers and mothers
are reading *Laddie* and *The Sick-a-Bed Lady,*
and their clergymen are preaching about *The
Inside of the Cup*—or the latest work dealing with the slums by some one who was
slum-born and slum-bred and is proud of it?
You can be slum-born and slum-bred and
still achieve something worth while; but it is
a stupid inverted snobbishness to be proud of
it. If one had a right to be proud of anything,
it would be of a continued decent tradition
back of one. The cultured person must have
put in a great many years with nothing to show
for it; his parents have usually put in a great
many years, for him, for which they have
nothing to show. There is nothing to show,
until you get the complex result of the discip-
lined and finished creature. "Culture" means a
long receptivity to things of the mind and the
spirit. There is no money in it; there is nothing
striking in it; there is in it no flattery of our
own time, or of the majority.

Ours is a commercial age, in which most
people are bent on getting money. That is a
platitude. It is also, intellectually speaking, a
materialistic age, when most of our intellectual
power is given either to prophylaxis, or to
industrial chemistry, or to the invention of
physical conveniences—all ultimately concerned

with the body. Even the philanthropists deal
with the soul through the body, and Christianity has long since become "muscular."
How, in such an age, can culture flourish—
culture, which cares even more about the spirit
than about the flesh? It was pointed out not
long ago, in an *Atlantic* article, that many of
our greatest minds have dwelt in bodies that
the eugenists would have legislated out of
existence. Many of the greatest saints found
sainthood precisely in denying the power of the
ailing flesh to restrict the soul. There is more
in the great mystics than psychiatry will ever
account for. But science, in spite of its vistas,
is short-sighted. It talks in æons, but keeps its
eye well screwed to the microscope. The geol-
ogic ages are dealt with by pick and hammer
and reduced to slides, and the lore of the stars
has become a pure matter of mathematical
formulæ. Human welfare is a question of
microbes. Neither pundit nor populace cares,
at the present day, for perspectives. The past
is discredited because it is not modern. Not to
be modern is the great sin.

So, perhaps, it is. But every one has, in his
day, been modern. And surely even modernity
is a poor thing beside immortality. Since we
must all die, is it not perhaps better to be a
dead lion than a living dog? And is it not a
crime against human nature to consider negligible "the best that has been thought and said

in the world"? It is only by considering it
negligible that we can consent to let ourselves
be overrun by the hordes of ignorance and
materialism — the people (God save the
mark!) of to-morrow. Let us stand, if we
must, on practical grounds: the bird in the
hand is worth two in the bush. As if our only
guaranty that to-morrow would be tolerable
were not precisely that it is sprung from a past
that we know to have been, at many points,
noble! It is pathetic to see people refusing to
learn the lessons of history; it is a waste that
no efficiency expert ought to permit. All learning is a textbook which would save much time
to him who works for the perfection of the
world. But I begin to think that our age does
not really care about perfection; and that it
would rather make a thousand-year-old mistake
than learn a remedy from history. So much the
worse for to-morrow!

But meanwhile let us—those of us who
can—see to it that the pre-eminent brains of
other ages shall not have passed away in vain.
M. Anatole France, in *La Révolte des
Anges*, has a good deal to say about the
absurdity of a Jehovah who still believes in
the Ptolemaïc system. Well, the Ptolemaïc system did not prevent the ancient world from
giving us Greek theatres and Roman law, or
England from giving us Magna Charta. We
are still imitating Greek theatres (rather

badly, I admit) in our stadia; Roman law is still, by and large, good enough for such an enlightened country as France; and Magna Charta—or its equivalent—had to be there before we could have a Declaration of Independence. Our superior scientific knowledge has not given us our standards of beauty or justice or liberty. Let us take what the present offers—airplanes and all. But let us not throw away what other men, in other ages, have died for the sake of discovering. If the lore of the past is useless, there is every chance—one must be very overweening indeed not to admit it— that the lore of our generation will be useless, too. Culture—whether you use the word itself or find another term—means only a decent economy of human experience. You cannot improve on things without keeping those things pretty steadily in mind. Otherwise you run the risk of wasting a lot of time doing something that has already been done. Any one, I think, will admit that. And it is not a far step to the realization that on the whole it is wise not to lose the past out of our minds. There is no glory in being wiser than the original savage; there is glory in being wiser than the original sage. But in order to be wiser than he, we must have a shrewd suspicion of how wise he was. By and large, without culture, that shrewd suspicion will never be ours.

FASHIONS IN MEN

NEVER, I fancy, has it been more true than it is today, that fiction reflects life. The best fiction has always given us a kind of precipitate of human nature—*Don Quixote* and *Tom Jones* are equally "true," and true, in a sense, for all time; but our modern books give us every quirk and turn of the popular ideal, and fifty years hence, if read at all, may be too "quaint" for words. And to any one who has been reading fiction for the last twenty years, it is cryingly obvious that fashions in human nature have changed.

My first novel was *Jane Eyre;* and at the age of eight, I fell desperately in love with Fairfax Rochester. No instance could serve better to point the distance we have come. I was not an extraordinary little girl (except that, perhaps, I was extraordinarily fortunate in being permitted to encounter the classics in infancy), and I dare say that if I had not met Mr. Rochester, I should have succumbed to some imaginary gentleman of a quite different stamp. It may be that I should have fallen in love—had time and chance permitted—with V. V. or The Beloved Vagabond. But I doubt it. In the first place, novels no longer

assume that it is the prime business of the
female heart (at whatever age) to surrender
itself completely to some man. Consequently,
the men in the novels of today are not calcu-
lated, as they once were, to hit the fluttering
mark. The emotions are the last redoubt to be
taken, as modern tactics direct the assault.

People are always telling us that fashions
in women have changed: what seems to me
almost more interesting is that fashions in men
(the stable sex) have changed to match. The
new woman (by which I mean the very newest) would not fall in love with Mr. Rochester. It is therefore "up to" the novelists to
create heroes whom the modern heroine will
fall in love with. This, to the popular satisfaction, they have done. And not only in fiction
have the men changed; in life, too, the men
of to-day are quite different. I know, because
my friends marry them.

It is immensely interesting, this difference.
One by one, the man has sloughed off his most
masculine (as we knew them) characteristics.
Gone are Mr. Rochester, who fought the duel
with the vicomte at dawn, and Burgo Fitzgerald (the only love of that incomparable
woman, Lady Glencora Palliser), who break-
fasted on curaçao and pâté de foie gras. No
longer does Blanche Ingram declare, "An English hero of the road would be the next best
thing to an Italian bandit, and that could only

be surpassed by a Levantine pirate." Blanche Ingram wants—and gets—the Humanitarian Hero: some one who has particular respect for convicts and fallen women, and whose favorite author is Tolstoï. He must qualify for the possession of her hand by long, voluntary residence in the slums; he may inherit ancestral acres only if he has, concerning them, socialistic intentions. He must be too altruistic to kill grouse, and if he is to be wholly up-to-date, he must refuse to eat them. He must never order "pistols and coffee": his only permitted weapon is benevolent legislation.

I do not mean that he is to be a milk-sop—"muscular Christianity" has at least taught us that it is well for the hero to be in the pink of condition, as he may any day have a street fight on his hands. And he should have the tongues of men and of angels. Gone is the inarticulate Guardsman—gone forever. The modern hero has read books that Burgo Fitzgerald and Guy Livingstone and Mr. Rochester never heard of. He is ready to address any gathering, and to argue with any antagonist, until dawn. He is, preferably, personally unconscious of sex until the heroine arrives; but he is by no means effeminate. He is a very complicated and interesting creature. Some mediæval traits are discernible in him; but the eighteenth century would not have known him for human.

What has he lost, this hero, and what has he gained? How did it all begin? In life, doubtless, it began with a feminine change of taste. Brilliant plumage has ceased to allure; and, I suspect, the peacock's tail, as much as the anthropoid ape's, is destined to elimination. We women of to-day are distrustful of the peacock's tail. We are mortally afraid of being misled by it, and of discovering, too late, that the peacock's soul is not quite the thing. Never has there been among the feminine young more scientific talk about sex, and never among the feminine young such a scientific distrust of it. Before a young woman suspects that she wants to marry a young man, she has probably discussed with him, exhaustively, the penal code, white slavery, eugenics, and race-suicide. The miracle—the everlasting miracle of Nature— is that she should want, in these circumstances, to marry him at all. She probably does not, unless his views have been wholly to her satisfaction. And with those views, what has the perpetual glory of the peacock's tail to do?

So much for life. In our English fiction, I am inclined to believe that George Eliot began it with Daniel Deronda. But, in our own day, Meredith did more. Up to the time of Meredith, the dominant male was the fashionable hero. Tom Jones, and Sir Charles Grandison, and Fairfax Rochester, and "Stunning" Warrington are as different as possible; but all of them, in their several ways, keep up one male tradition in fiction. It is within our own day that that tradition has entirely changed. Have you ever noticed how inveterately, in Meredith's novels, the schoolmaster or his spiritual kinsman comes out on top? Lord Ormont cannot stand against Matey Weyburn, Lord Fleetwood against Owain Wythan, Sir Willoughby Patterne against Vernon Whitford. The little girl who fell in love with Mr. Rochester would have preferred any one of these gentlemen (yes, even Sir Willoughby!) to his rival; but I dare say the event would have proved her wrong. Certainly the wisdom of the ladies' choice was never doubtful to Meredith himself. The soldier and the aristocrat cannot endure the test they are put to by the sympathetic male with a penchant for the enfranchised woman. Vain for Lord Ormont to accede to Aminta's taste for publicity; vain for Lord Fleetwood to become the humble wooer of Carinthia Jane: each has previously been convicted of pride.

Now, in an earlier day, no woman would have looked at a man who was not proud—who was not, even, a little too proud. Pride, by which Lucifer fell, was the chief hall-mark of the gentleman. Moreover, in that earlier day, women did not expect their heroes to explain everything to them: a certain amount of reticence, a measure of silence, was also one of the hall-marks of the gentleman. If a bit of mystery could be thrown in, so much the better. It gave her something to exercise her imagination on. Think of the Byronic males—Conrad, Lara, and the rest! If they had told all, where would they have been? Think of Lovelace and Heathcliff and Darcy and Brian de Bois Guilbert!

Heroes, once, were always disdaining to speak, and spurning their foes. Nowadays, no hero disdains to speak, and no hero ventures to spurn anyone—least of all, his foes. He is humble of heart and very loquacious. Mrs. Humphry Ward has inherited from George Eliot; and the latest heroes of Mr. Galsworthy and Mr. Hewlett, for example, are the children of Vernon Whitford, Matey Weyburn, and Owain Wythan (of whom it is not explicitly written that they had any others). They are humanitarian and democratic; they are ignorant of hatred; they are inclined to think the ill-born necessarily better than the well-born; and they are quite sure that women are superior to men. True, Mr. Galsworthy always seems to be looking backward; he never forgets the ancient tradition that he is combating. His young aristocrats who eschew the ways of aristocracy are unhappy, and virtue in their case is "its only reward." Perhaps that is why his novels always leave us with the medicinal taste of inconclusion in our mouths.

[99]

But take a handful of heroes elsewhere: the Reverend John Hodder, the ex-convict "Daniel Smith," V. V., or even Coryston, the Socialist peer. Where, in a lot of them, do you find either pride or reticence in the old sense? Where, in any one of them, do you find the Satanic charm? Which one would Harriet Byron, or Jane Eyre, or Catherine Earnshaw, or Elizabeth Bennett, have looked at with eyes of love?

The "Satanic charm." The phrase is out. Milton, I suspect, is responsible for the tradition that has lasted so long, and is now being broken utterly to pieces. Milton made Satan delightful, and our good Protestant novelists for a long time followed his lead, in that they gave their delightful men some of the Satanic traits. Proud they were and scornfully silent, as we have recalled; and conventional to the last degree. "Conventional," that is, in the stricter sense; by which it is not meant that as portraits they were unconvincing, or that, as men, they never offended Mrs. Grundy. They were conventional in that they followed a convention; in that they were, to a large extent, predicable. They were jealous of their honor, and believed it vindicable by the duel; they had no doubt that good women were better than bad, and that pedigree in human beings was as important as pedigree in animals; and though they might be quixotic on occasion, they were not democratic *pour deux sous*. The barmaid was not their sister, nor the stevedore their brother. (The Satan of *Paradise Lost,* as we all remember, was a splendid snob.)

Moreover, they were sophisticated—and not merely out of books. The Faust idea, having prevailed for many centuries, has at last been abandoned—and perhaps, our sober sense may tell us, rightly; but not so long ago there was still something more repellent to the female imagination about the man who chose not to know, than about the man who chose not to abstain. I do not mean that we were supposed always to be looking for a Tom Jones or a Roderick Random—we might be looking for a Sir Charles Grandison, no less; but at least, when we found our hero, we expected to find him wiser than we. Nowadays, a girl rather likes to give a man points—and often (in fiction, at least) has to. Meredith railed against the "veiled virginal doll" as heroine. Well: our heroines now are never veiled virginal dolls; but sometimes our heroes are. Lancelot has gone out, and Galahad has come in. I suspect that there is a literary law of compensation, and that, Ibsen and Strindberg to the contrary notwithstanding, there has to be a veiled virginal doll somewhere in a really taking romance. Perhaps it is fair that the sterner sex should have its turn at guarding ideals by the hearthstone, while women make the grand tour.

Let me not be misunderstood. I am not

referring particularly to that knowledge which any man is better without, but to the Odyssean experience which, in their respective measures, heroes were wont to have behind them:

> 'And saw the cities, and the counsels knew
>
> .   .   .   .
>
> Of many men, and many a time at sea
> Within his heart he bore calamity.'

They had at least seen the towns and the minds of men, and their morals were the less likely to be upset by a conventional assault upon them. Does any one chance to remember, I wonder, Theron Ware, led to his "damnation" by his first experience of a Chopin nocturne? It would have taken more than a Chopin nocturne to make any of our seasoned heroes do something that he did not wish to. They knew something of society, and *ergo* of women; they had experienced, directly or vicariously, human romance; and they had read history. Nowadays, they are apt to know little or nothing—to begin with—of society, women, or romance, except what may be got from brand-new books on sociology; and they pride themselves on knowing no history. History, with its eternal stresses and selections, is nothing if not aristocratic, and our heroes nowadays must be democratic or they die. It is an age of complete faith in the superiority of the lower classes—the swing of the pendulum, no doubt, from the other extreme of thinking the lower classes morally and æsthetically negligible. "Privilege" is as detestable now in matters of intellect and breeding as in matters of finance and politics. The man with the muckrake has got past the office into the drawing-room. If your hero has the bad luck not to have been born in the slums, he must at least have the wit to take up his habitation there as soon as he comes of age. We have learned that riches are corrupting, but (except in the special sense of vice-commission reports) we have not yet learned that poverty is rather more corrupting than wealth.

Sophistication, whether social, intellectual, or æsthetic, is now the deadly sin. If we are sophisticated, we may not be good enough for Ellis Island. And there goes another of the hall-marks of the gentleman as he was once known to fiction. Our hero in old days might not have condescended to the glittering assemblies of fashion, but there was never any doubt that, if he had, he would, in spite of himself, have been king of his company as soon as he entered the room. He might have been hard up, but his necktie would not have been "a black sea holding for life a school of fat white fish." He might have been lonely or gloomy, but he would not have been diffident, and he would never, never, *never* have "blinked" at the heroine. "My godlike friend had carelessly

put his hair-brush into the butter," says Asti-
cot, at the outset, of the Beloved Vagabond.
Now in picaresque novels, we were always
meeting people who did that sort of thing; but
they were not gentlemen. Whereas, the Beloved Vagabond is of noble birth, and despite
his ten years' abeyance, finds the countess quite
ready to marry him. She does not marry him
in the end, to be sure, but we are permitted to
feel that there was something lacking in her
because Paragot's manners at tea did not
please her. The hero of old had what used to
be called "a sense of fitness," and a saving sense
of humor, which combined to prevent his entering a ballroom as John the Baptist. The same
lucky combination would have prevented him—
in literature, at least—from wooing the millionaire's child with dusty commonplaces of the
Higher Criticism or jeremiads against the
daughters of Heth. But perhaps millionaires'
children today take that sort of thing for
manners. To the argument that a performance
of the kind takes courage, one can only reply
that, judging from the enthusiasm with which
the preaching hero is received by the heroine,
it apparently does not. And in any case, the
hero is too sublimely ignorant of what socially
constitutes courage to deserve any credit for it.

Sometimes, of course, like Mr. Galsworthy's
men, he perceives, with some inherited sense,
that his kind of thing is not likely to be wel-

comed; and then he goes sadly and sternly away, leaving the girl to accept a wooer with more technique. But usually he cuts out everybody. For the chief hall-mark of a gentleman, now, is the desire to reform his own class out of all recognition.

Women, as we know, have long wanted to be talked to as if they were men; and the result is that heroines now let themselves be lectured at in a way that very few men would endure. Alison Parr marries the Rev. John Hodder, and Carlisle Heth would have married V. V. if he had lived. Well: Clara Middleton married Vernon Whitford, and Carinthia Jane married Owain Wythan, and Aminta married Matey Weyburn.

I may have seemed to be speaking cynically. That, I can give my word of honor, I am not. It is well that we have come to realize that there are some adventures which, in themselves, add no lustre to a man's name. It is well that we take thought for the lower strata of humanity—though our actual reforms, I fancy, show their authors as taking thought not for to-morrow but for to-day. Certainly brutality, or the indifference which is negative brutality, is not a beautiful or a moral thing; and certainly we do not particularly sympathize with Thackeray shedding tears as he went away from his publishers because they had obliged him to save Pendennis's chastity.

That dreadful person, Arthur Pendennis, would surely not have been made any less dreadful by being permitted to seduce Fanny Bolton.

It is right to think of the poor; it is right to bend our energies, as citizens, to the economic bettering of their lot. No one could sanely regret our doing so. But there is always danger in saying the thing which is not, and in pretending that because some virtues have hitherto not been recognized, the virtues that have been recognized are no good. One sympathizes with Towneley (in that incomparable novel *The Way of All Flesh*) when Ernest asks him:

" 'Don't you like poor people very much yourself?'

"Towneley gave his face a comical but good-natured screw and said quietly, but slowly and decidedly, 'No, no, no,' and escaped.

"Of course, some poor people were very nice, and always would be so, but as though scales had fallen suddenly from his eyes he saw that no one was nicer for being poor, and that between the upper and lower classes there was a gulf which amounted practically to an impassable barrier."

It is a great pity that Samuel Butler did not live longer and write more novels. But in regretting him, we shall do well to remember that though publication was delayed until some time after the author's death, the bulk of *The*

Way of All Flesh was written in the '70's. *The Way of All Flesh* is not sympathetic to the contemporary mood; it is one of those books so much ahead of its time (except perhaps in ecclesiastical matters) that the time has not yet caught up with it. It was doomed inevitably to an interval of oblivion. The case reminds one of *Richard Feverel.*

Only in one way is *The Way of All Flesh* quite contemporary. The hero thinks so well of the prostitute that he marries her. On the other hand, to be sure, he bitterly regrets it, which is not contemporary. I do not mean that the hero's marrying her is especially in the literary fashion, but his thinking well of her is. You will notice that in our moral fever we do not leave the prostitute out of our novels— no, indeed: she must be there to give spice, as of old. Only now, instead of being entangled with her, the young gentleman preaches to her; and she loves him for it. Perhaps this is what happens nowadays in real life. I do not pretend to know; but I suspect it is true, for I fancy the only kind of person who could invent the contemporary plot is the kind who would live it. The wildest imaginings of the people who are made differently would hardly stretch to it. And not only does the hero find himself immensely touched by the tragedy of the disreputable woman—which is, after all, in certain cases plausible enough—he burns to introduce his fiancée to her. Now that, again, may be life—Mr. Winston Churchill, for example, should know better than I—but it is certainly a world with the sense of values gone wrong. And when we have lost our sense of values, we shall presently lose the values as well. The girl herself is often to blame: did not the fiancée of Simon de Gex go of her own initiative to see the animal-tamer, and come away to renounce him, convinced that the animal-tamer was the nobler woman? Which, emphatically, she was not. But then, as we know from long experience of Mr. Locke, he cannot keep his head with circus-people about; and sawdust is incense to him. Let Mr. Locke have his little foibles by all means; but even Mr. Locke should not have made the spoiled darling of society marry the animal-tamer (one side of her face having been nearly clawed off) and *then* go with her into city missionary work. Yet I do not believe it is really Mr. Locke's fault. The public at present loves as a sister the woman with a past; and loves city missionary work, if possible, more.

The fact is that with all our imitation of Meredith—and every one who is not imitating Tolstoï is imitating Meredith—he has failed to save us. We have taken all his prescriptions blindly—except one. We have emancipated our women and emasculated our men; we have cast down the mighty from their seats and exalted them of low degree; we have learned all the Radical shibboleths and say them for our morning prayers; and we have faced the fact of sex so squarely that we can hardly see anything else. But we have not learned his saving hatred of the sentimentalist. Miss May Sinclair has admirably pointed out in her study of the three Brontës that Charlotte Brontë was exceedingly modern in her detestation of sentimentality. Modern she may have been— with Meredith; but not modern with the present novelists, for they are almost too sentimental to be endured. And there is the whole trouble. We think Thackeray an old fool for being sentimental over Amelia Sedley; but how does it better the case to be sentimental, instead, over the heroine of *The Promised Land?* Amelia Sedley was all in all a much nicer person, if not half so clever. She may have snivelled a good deal, but she was capable of loving some one else better than herself.

Of course, I have cited only a few instances —those that happened to come most easily to mind. But let any reader of fiction run over mentally a group of contemporary heroes, and see if the substitutions I have named have not pretty generally taken place. Has not pride given way to humility, reticence to glibness, class-consciousness to a wild democracy, the code of manners to an uncouth unworldliness, and honor in the old sense to a burning pas-

sion for reform—"any old" reform? Do not
these men lead us into the heterogeneous company of the unclassed of both sexes—and ask
us to look upon them as saints in motley? Has
not the world of fiction changed in the last
twenty years? The hero in old days sometimes
fell foul of the law by getting into debt. But
we were not supposed, therefore, to be on his
side against the law. Now, the hero does not,
perhaps, get into legal difficulties himself, but
he is always passionately on the side of the
people whom laws were devised to protect the
respectable from. The scientific tendency to
consider that aristocracy consists merely in
freedom from certain physical taints has permeated fiction. "Is not one man as good as
another?" asked the demagogue. "Of course
he is, and a great deal better!" replied the
excited Irishman in the crowd. We are in the
thick of a popular mania for thinking all the
undesirables "a good deal better." The modern
hero is, to my mind, in intention, if not in
execution, an admirable figure; and though one
rather expects him any day to give his whole
fortune for a gross of green spectacles, one
will not, for that, find him any less likable.
Some day he will rediscover the Dantesque
hierarchy of souls implicit in humanity. And
then, perhaps, he will get back his charm.

Some one is probably bursting to observe
that we have a school of realists at hand; and
that no one can accuse Mr. Wells and Mr.

Bennett of sentimentality—also that we have Mr. Shaw and Mr. Granville Barker and Mr. Masefield as mounted auxiliaries in the field. I grant Mr. Bennett; I am not so sure about Mr. Wells. But certainly Mr. Wells is not sentimental as Mr. William de Morgan, Mr. Winston Churchill, Mr. Meredith Nicholson, Mr. Theodore Dreiser, Mr. H. S. Harrison, and Miss Ellen Glasgow are sentimental. If he is sentimental at all, it is rather over ideas than people. (Mr. Masefield, I am inclined to think, is simply catering to the special audience that Thomas Hardy, by his silence, has left gaping and empty.) Let us look into the matter a little. "Sentimental" is one of the most difficult catchwords in the world to define; and you can get a roomful of intelligent people quarrelling over it any time. Perhaps, for our purposes, it will serve merely to say that the sentimentalist is always, in one way or another, disloyal to facts. He cannot be trusted to give a straight account, because his own sense of things is more valuable to him than the truth. He has come in on the top of the pragmatic wave, and the sands of Anglo-Saxondom are strewn thick with him. He serves, in Kipling's phrase, the God of Things as They Ought to Be (according to his private feeling). His own perversion may be æsthetic, or intellectual, or moral, or sociological, but he is always recognizable by his tampering with truth.

Now, Mr. Wells does tamper with truth.

He did it, for example, in the case of Ann
Veronica. He wanted Ann Veronica to be a
nice girl under twenty, and he wanted her,
even more, to be unduly awakened to certain
physical aspects of sex. It was sentimentality
that made him draw her as he did: determina-
tion to prove that the girl who loved as he
wanted her to love was just as conventional as
any one else. You cannot have your cake and
eat it too; but the sentimentalist blindly refuses
to accept that. Accordingly, we get the unconvincing creature that Mr. Wells wanted to
believe existed. Mr. Wells's heroes may not
seem to bear out my argument so well as Mr.
Galsworthy's. To be sure, Mr. Wells is not so
sentimental as Mr. Galsworthy, and he has
not, like the author of *The Man of Property,* and *Fraternity,* and *Justice,* one—just
one—fixed idea. Mr. Galsworthy always deals
with a man who is in love with some other
man's wife; and his world is thereby nar-
rowed. Mr. Wells is interested in a good many
things, and his politics are not purely philanthropic as most of our novelists' politics
are. But Mr. Wells's heroes, even when they
are fairly fortunate, are pre-occupied with their
own notions of sociological duty, even more
than they are pre-occupied with passion, though
their passion is "special" enough when it
comes. Would any one except a Wells hero
take a trip to India and come away having

seen nothing but the sweat-shops of Bombay?
Always the author's sympathy is with the
under dog; whether it is Kipps or Mr.
Polly living out his long foredoomed existence, or
George Ponderevo analyzing Bladesover with
diabolic keenness and aching contempt. "I'm a
spiritual guttersnipe in love with unimaginable
goddesses," says Ponderevo in a burst of
frankness. There you have the Wells hero to
the life. And Mr. Bennett's people are only
spiritual guttersnipes who are *not* in love with
unimaginable goddesses.

The point is that the guttersnipe is having
his turn in fiction: if our American heroes are
not guttersnipes themselves, it is their sign of
grace to be supremely interested in guttersnipes. In one way or the other, the guttersnipe must have his proper prominence. Of
course, there are differences and degrees: a
few heroes get no nearer the lower classes
than a passionate desire for reform tickets and
municipal sanitation. But ordinarily they must
go through Ernest Pontifex's state of believing
that poor people are not only more important,
but in every way way nicer than rich people;
and few of them go back utterly on that
belief, as Ernest did. Perhaps that, more than
anything else, marks the change of fashion in
men. For gentlemen were always, in their way,
benevolent; but formerly they had not achieved
the paradox that the object of benevolence is

ex officio more interesting than the bestower.
I said earlier that in life, as well as in
literature, men had changed. One's instances,
obviously, must be from books, and not from
one's acquaintance; but I spoke truth. Philanthropy is the latest social ladder, but it would
not be so if the people on the top rung were
not interested in philanthropy. There has been,
for whatever reason, a tremendous spurt of
interest in sociological questions. Our hard-
headed young men, of high ideals, find themselves fighting, of necessity, on a different
battlefield from any that strategists would have
chosen thirty years ago. Moreover, philanthropy being woman's way into politics, women
have been giving their calm, or hysterical,
attention to problems which, thirty years since,
did not, as problems, exist for them. I said
that the change of taste in women would probably account for much of the change of fashion
in men. A schoolmate of mine, writing me
some years since of her engagement, said (in
nearly these words), "He is tremendously interested in city missionary work; it wouldn't
have been quite perfect if we hadn't had that
in common." Both were spoiled darlings of
fortune, but the statement was quite sincere.
Undoubtedly, without that, it would not have
been "quite perfect" in the eyes of either.
The mere conversation of the marriageable
young has changed past belief. "Social service"

has usurped so many subjects! Have many people stopped to realize, I wonder, how completely the psychological novel and the "problem" play (in the old sense) have gone out of date? The psychology of hero and heroine, their emotional attitudes to each other, are largely worked out now in terms of their attitudes to impersonal questions, their religious or their sociological "principles." The individual personal reaction counts less and less. If they agree on the same panacea for the social evils, the author can usually patch up a passion sufficient for them to marry on. Gone, for the most part, are the pages of intimate analysis. No intimate analysis is needed any longer. As for the "problem play," we have it still with us, but in another form. *The Doll's House* and *The Second Mrs. Tanqueray* are both antiquated: we do not call a drama a problem play now unless it preaches a new kind of legislation. And as for sex—in its finer aspects it no longer interests us.

There was a great deal more sex, in its subtler manifestations, in the old novels and plays, than in the new ones. Not so long ago, a novel was a love-story; and it was of supreme importance to a hero whether or not he could make the heroine care for him. It was also of supreme importance to the heroine. The romance was all founded on sex; and yet sex was hardly mentioned. Our heroes and

heroines still marry; but when they consider
sex at all, they are apt to consider it biologic-
ally, not romantically. We, as a public, are
more frankly interested in sex than ever; but
we think of it objectively, and a little brutally,
in terms of demand and supply. And so we get
often the pathetic spectacle of the hero and
heroine having no time to make love to each
other in the good old-fashioned way, because
they are so busy suppressing the red-light dis-
trict and compiling statistics of disease. Much
of the frankness, doubtless, is a good thing;
but, beyond a doubt, it has cheapened passion.
For passion among civilized people is a subtle
thing; it is wrapped about with dreams and
imaginings, and can bring human beings to
salvation as well as to perdition. But when it
is shown to us as the mere province of cour-
tesans, small wonder that we turn from it to
the hero who will have difficulty in feeling or
inspiring it. Especially since we are told, at
the same time, that even the courtesan plies
her trade only from direst necessity.

After all, the only safe person to fall in love
with nowadays *is* a reformer: socially, financially, and sentimentally. And most women, at
least, could (if they would) say with the Prin-
cesse Mathilde, "Je n'aime que les romans
dont je voudrais être l'héroïne." Certainly,
unless for some special reason, no novel of
which one would not like to be the heroine—in

love with the hero—will reach the hundred thousand mark. If there are any of us left who regret the gentlemen of old—who still prefer our Darcy or even our Plantagenet Palliser— we must write our own novels, and divine our own heroes under the protective coloring of their conventional breeding. For they are not being "featured," at present, either in life or in literature.

THE NEWEST WOMAN

IT was the late George Meredith, if I mistake not, who was credited with bringing women into their joint inheritance of wit and passion. He himself supposed himself to discard, first of the novelists, the "veiled virginal doll." The *jeune fille* had, in the course of the late eighteenth and early nineteenth centuries, become somewhat dehumanized. She was far, indeed, from the frank heroines of Shakespeare, to whom every year was leap year. The heroine of the old-fashioned sentimental novel forsook her blushing, fainting, tear-shedding, letter-writing girlhood, only to become, on her wedding day, the British matron. There seems to have been no transition. Meredith apparently felt that the feminine share in romance was deplorably and inaccurately minimized. He exaggerated, perhaps. Scott gave us a few fine examples of the beautiful girl without frill or flutter, who was aware of her own mind. George Eliot knew a thing or two about her sex; and Jane Eyre, in her day, was notoriously explicit.

Not long since, indeed, having brought myself quite up to date with the fiction of the contemporary English school—even to the last instalments of its serial novels—I sought out the most *démodé* of the English novelists. "Let me see," I murmured to myself, "just what it is that we have thought it worth while, at this expense, to escape." Accordingly, I procured all the volumes of *Sir Charles Grandison.* Nothing, it seemed, could be fairer than to go to Richardson; and, in all the work of Richardson, fairest, surely, to go to *Sir Charles.*

I have never known any one who was ashamed to confess that *Sir Charles Grandison* bored him. It is the last work which any defender of the old school of fiction would think of using as a basis for argument. And yet, even in that epic of priggery, the natural note is not wholly lacking. Harriet Byron loved Sir Charles while he was still bound to the Lady Clementina, and bore herself with dignity when her friends cautioned her against her own feeling. "If this should end at last in love" (she writes), "and I should be *entangled in a hopeless passion,* the object of it would be Sir Charles Grandison: he could not insult me; and mean as the word *pity* in some cases sounds, I had rather have his pity than the love of any other man." Such a cry, even Richardson, with all his prurient prudishness, could give us.

Yet we must give Meredith his due; and Meredith, on the whole, honestly surpasses these others in the shining list of his adoring heroines—adoring with such dominance in meekness, such gayety in surrender. Rose Jocelyn, Henrietta Fakenham, Aminta Farrell, Clare Doria Forey (let us write it in full, for so she liked it best), Cecilia Halkett, Janet Ilchester—it would be hard to match, within the century, that group of girls.

All these names have been recalled simply as witnesses to the fact that there is—in spite of the contentions of the contemporary novelists—a perfectly consistent tradition, in English novels, of the frank young woman. It is of the first importance to establish this, for these contemporary authors are talking as if their Anns and Isabels and Hildas were the only *jeunes filles* who had ever dared, in literature, to love as spirited girls in life really do. Just here one quarrels with their pretensions. The Victorian convention may have given us Amelia Sedley, and Lucy Desborough, and Lily Dale; but the Victorian era gave us also Catherine Earnshaw, and Jane Eyre, and Eustacia Vye. Our contemporaries are doing nothing new when they show us the *jeune fille* falling in love before she is proposed to; they are doing nothing new when they show us the *jeune fille* wishing, quite specifically, to be a wife; they are not even doing anything new— rather, something quite *dix-huitième* and *rococo*—when they show us the *jeune fille* considering whether she will put up with being a

mistress. The *jeune fille* glorying in her choice
of the illicit relation is something, let us grant
them, more nearly new. Yet how they gabble,
upon their peak in Darien!

No; these authors have not broken with the
Victorian convention — that simple acrobatic
feat demanded of all beginners. But they have
broken with the laboratory method. If they
think that in Ann Veronica, in Hilda Lessways,
in Isabel Rivers, they have been more accurate
than their great predecessors, they are quite
simply mistaken. I am not proposing to myself,
or to any one else, to be shocked by these
young women. Being shocked leaves one, in
the world of criticism, with no retort. Whether
or not one is shocked by them is quite another
question, and one that does not come into this
discussion. My own objection to the school of
Mr. Shaw, Mr. Wells, and Mr. Bennett, is
that their heroines are not convincing.

There is a great deal said and written, nowadays, about women as they are and as they
ought to be; and very little of it is in the tone
of *Sesame and Lilies*. We are told very con-
tradictory things about our sex; and we are
exhorted with unvarying earnestness to believe
each contradiction. We are jeered at for being
Nietzschean Anns, embodying the ruthless life-
force, pursuing the man that we may have
children by him. We are also preached at for
causing race-suicide. We must want children

more than anything else in the world; and we must want the state to take care of them for us after they are born. We must return to the Stone Age; and we must, at the same time, join the Fabian Society. We must submit to the intense conservatism of eugenics; but we must, on the other hand, insult Mrs. Grundy, whenever we find it convenient, by taking lovers instead of husbands. We ought not to marry without assurance that our children will be physically perfect; but we may not expose them on a mountain top if by any chance they are not.

Only the pragmatist (be it said in passing), with his avowed power of sucking the truth simultaneously from two mutually exclusive hypotheses, could do all the things that, with authority, we are told to do. "Modern, indeed! She" (Ann Veronica) "was going to be as primordial as chipped flint." Yet, if we accept the chronologies of history (which seems sane enough) nothing could be more "modern" than Ann Veronica's way of being pre-historic. Perhaps the solution is for all women to become pragmatists? Some of us are bewildered by all this; and we wonder a little if the heart-breaking medley of preachments is not the fruit of that antique and unpardonable sin—*mêler les genres.* In all this chaos, one thing seems to be generally agreed on: women are, contrary to fusty tradition, very like men—whether like

them according to *L'Age Dangereux,* or like
them according to the latest suffrage pamphlet.
That is the only thing that we shall unfailingly
be told.

There is something in it. We *are* more like
men than Mrs. Radcliffe would have believed.
But the method chosen by these modern heroines of being like men is chiefly, it would
appear, to be more so. They will not go half-
way, but three quarters. The old-fashioned
man sometimes relented. The new-fashioned
woman makes quick work of her lover's virtue.
There is hardly a villain in an old play but
would have let the lady off, if she had pleaded
with him as Capes pleads with Ann Veronica.
The qualms, the scruples, the regrets, are all
the man's: the girl refuses utterly to indulge in
anything so weak. Capes is unfortunate enough
to say something to Ann Veronica about honor.
"Only your queer code of honor—Honor!
Once you begin with love you have to see it
through." Away with inhibitions!

"But," some one will object, "all this has
been said before. And literature is full of
women who prey passionately on the men they
say they love. They are a recognized type."
Granted; but until now, the passionate preying
and the unsought soliciting have not been done
by the young unmarried girl of respectable
traditions. The type is represented, from Poti-
phar's wife down, by the woman who is no

longer *jeune fille*. One has not traversed either literature or life without hearing of exceptions. But they are exceptions. The point is, not that young women have hitherto been restrained by religion and convention, and that when they become free-thinkers and despise the existing order, they express themselves as they really are. The point is that they really are not, for the most part, like Ann Veronica and Hilda Lessways.

I and my friends do not object to Ann and Hilda because we are afraid that, if we do not, people will think that we are like that. We object to them because we are told that they are normal, healthy-minded young women who have led perfectly respectable lives on the borders, at least, of gentility; and because we know that normal, healthy-minded young women who have lived such lives do not approach their first love affairs in the temper of these heroines. If you wish to say that the authors are merely discussing pathological cases, you will to some extent be letting them out, but they will not thank you for it. What is perfectly clear is that they believe girls of eighteen or twenty are like that. The last thing that they think, evidently, is that these young ladies need any attention from physicians or alienists. They think—God save the mark!— that they have described, in each case, a really nice girl. Up to a certain point, Ann Veronica *is* nice. When she falls in love, her author goes back on her disgracefully. He does not go back on her by making her horrid: he goes back on her by destroying her actuality.

One is ready to grant, I say, that women are more like men than some—not all—of the old-fashioned novelists would have had us believe. Let us rail, by all means, at the "veiled virginal doll." Let us disagree with Tolstoï (it is always good to disagree with Tolstoï!) when he says, in the *Sonate de Kreutzer,* "une jeune fille pure ne veut pas un amant; elle veut des enfants." Let us admit that the modern girl really is frank with herself about her desire to marry the man she has chosen. Indeed, I cannot think who will deny it. But there our respect for realism bids us stop. It is a complex and misty matter, this probing of the young girl's secret attitude to life and her lover.

Perhaps the greatest blunder of the new realists is that they do not see how complex and misty it is. The whole question is almost impossible of discussion, it is so difficult and delicate. Record the images in the girl's mind, if you must—that is the exhaustive, exhausting rule of realism. But for God's sake, record them as vague, since vague they are! These authors fail, precisely because they must, at each instant, be vivid. One is tempted to recall to them Mr. Chesterton's difficulty with Browning's biography: "One can make a map of a labyrinth, but who can make a map of a mist?" Mr. Wells and Mr. Bennett are, apparently, the successful cabmen who can. They offer to take you anywhere you like in this London fog of the girl's mind. Under their fitful guidance, you will get somewhere; but it may not be the address you gave them.

It is time to come to instances. Luckily for one's contention, the frank young feminine thing is, in spite of a few sentimental aberrations of a century ago, in the great English literary tradition. (What the new novelists have given us, one might remark, is more like the frank young thing crossed with the highwayman.) No one need be more explicit than Juliet in desiring possession of the man she loves, but even Juliet does not find her passion for Romeo summing itself up in Ann Veronica's desire to kiss her idol's feet because she is sure that they must have the firm texture of his hands; nor is she overpowered at every turn, like Hilda, by his "faint, exciting, masculine odor." And, surely, if any one were to bring up an explicit heroine, it would be the Nurse! Romantic lovers have always prayed for union. Long since, Sir Thomas Browne said, "United souls are not satisfied with embraces, but desire to be truly each other; which, being impossible, their desires are infinite, and must proceed without a possibility of satisfaction." What lover has not known that hurt? What lover, man or woman, has not welcomed marriage, and, at the same time, thought it a *pis-aller?* The notion is not a new one. It has never been in the greatest tradition of poetry or of life for the woman who loves to hold back.

That is not our quarrel with these misrepresented heroines. Our quarrel with them is that, being misrepresented themselves, they misrepresent their prototypes. It is a matter chiefly, perhaps, of the actual content of their minds. The visions of experience are not the visions of inexperience; moreover, there is not one frank young thing in ten thousand who does not wrap her ardor in a blessed cloak of vagueness. She may laugh at her faint atavistic shiver; but she feels it. She may immensely like the feeling of her lover's arms about her; but she does not instinctively set herself to imagining details that only the slow processes of intimacy will normally familiarize her with. She may glory in his total effect of physical perfection; but she does not go over his "points," as if she were buying a horse, or drawing an athlete in a life-class. Imagine Chaucer's feelings, if any one had tried to confound Emilye with the Wife of Bath! Yet it is something very like that which Mr. Bennet has done in his analysis of Hilda's psychology during the momentous half-hour before she becomes engaged to Cannon.

"But at the same time she was in the small hot room, and both George Cannon's hands were on her unresisting shoulders; and then they were round her, and she felt his physical nearness, the texture of his coat and of his skin; she could see in a mist the separate hairs of his tremendous moustache and the colors swimming in his eyes; her nostrils expanded in alarm to a faint exciting masculine odor. She was disconcerted, if not panicstruck, by the violence of his first kiss; but her consternation was delectable to her."

Every woman and most men know, I fancy, that if Hilda's first proximity to the man who dominated her imagination was of precisely that nature, her reaction was probably not precisely of that sort. Even the impersonal machinery of the psychological laboratory would have registered in her a distinct recoil. The microscope is not, and never has been, the lover's favorite instrument. It is doubtful if even the man himself would have been allured by the accurate and intimate perception of the coarseness of his beloved's skin. One thinks a little, in spite of one's self, of Gulliver and Glumdalclitch. Certain it is—and rather amusing, all things considered—that none of the men in these novels indulges in the sensations that crowd the heroines' hours; though it is written of nearly all the heroes that they had experienced matrimony, at the least. May it not be that the authors know their own sex better than ours? Granted that women are very like men: can one justly, on that hypothesis, show them as more scornful of conventions, of codes of honor, of every reticence, moral, intellectual, and physical, than these men whom they consider their masters? It is in each case the man who has the bad quarters of an hour over their common breaches, real or fancied, of loyalty and decency and public opinion; the man who has, for his own peace, to find a philosophy that justifies them both.

These authors are not alone among contemporaries in recording such heightened moments of a girl's life. One calls to mind, for the sheer similarity of the mental plight, Elizabeth, in *The Iron Woman*. Thus Elizabeth writes to David:

" 'Dear' (she stopped to kiss the paper), 'dear, I hope you won't burn it up because I am tired of waiting, and I hope you are too';— when she wrote those last words, she was suddenly shy; 'Uncle is to give me the money on my birthday—let us be married that day. I *want* to be married. I am all yours, David, all my soul, and all my mind, and all my body. I have nothing that is not yours to take; so the money is yours. No, I will not even give it to you! it belongs to you already—as I do. Dear, come and take it—and me. I love you—love you—love you. *I want you to take me.* I want to be your wife. Do you understand? I *want* to belong to you. I *am* yours.'

"So she tried, this untutored creature, to put her soul and body into words, to write the thing that cannot even be spoken, whose utterance is silence."

There is no need to follow further Mrs. Deland's analysis of the situation: the proud and practical reply from David, which the girl considers a rebuff; her sudden marrying of the man she does not love—as sheer expression of outraged modesty, and recoil from the man who had not known how to treat her confession. There would be no wisdom in comparing *The Iron Woman,* from any other point of view, with the novels we have been mentioning. This one episode is interesting simply as a different and more convincing record of the frank young thing's relation to her own frankness, and of the fiery limits of that frankness; pages of racking accuracy, in which the girl nearly dies of the memory of her own explicitness. One has not even power to protest against Elizabeth's tragic and foolish act in marrying Blair; it follows upon that mood with the raw inevitability of life.

Some adherents of the new school may think it indelicate to base a general accusation on the single point of the heroine's psychology. In the first place, the accusation is not so general as to preclude very definite admiration of other aspects of the school's achievement. There is much in Mr. Wells's *New Machiavelli* besides the hero's affair with Isabel Rivers; much that goes to the mind and heart of all of us. As for effectiveness of method and brilliancy of style—one simply does not see the need of adding one piping voice to the harmonious and already deafening chorus. Were there the need, one would do it.

But the contemporary school has set out to "do" a new type of woman: a type which it considers important, if not dominant. It has even the air of saying: "This is the kind of girl with whom intelligent men in the immediate future will have overwhelmingly (and to their salvation!) to deal. Behold the Newest Woman."

The *crux* in each book, for the average reader, is the maturing of the relation between the man and the girl. The girl exists only, in spite of her intellectual qualities, for the sake of that relation. In each case, she is the ideal mate, the high exponent of her sex. She deserves, and must bear, serious consideration from every point of view. One has chosen the realistic point of view because realism is the method these authors abide by. They aim at telling the truth as it is; therefore, they stand

or fall by the accuracy of their vivid and multitudinous detail. We are not in the pulpit, but
in the laboratory. One's honest impression is
that the scientific observers have mixed their
slides.

It is one thing to make your heroine believe
in free love—doubtless many women do. It is
pardonable to science to exhibit exceptions to
the feminine rule, in the person of the girl
initially over-sexed or neurotic: such cases are
known to other scientists than these. But it is
quite another thing to insist on the niceness,
the normality, the uninterruptedly respectable
and uneventful breeding of a girl—to exhibit
her as the type, in other words—and then
credit her with reactions that do not belong to
the type.

There is no point in preaching against a
modern spirit that is going to develop Anns
and Hildas and Isabels *ad libitum*. The conception of them as heroines may be a sign of
the times; but they themselves are not yet
numerous enough to be a sign of the times. It
is even doubtful if novelists can do in a decade
what Nature has never shown any sign of
doing in all her lazy evolutionary progress:
completely alter natural feminine instincts.
"But the worst of Ann Veronica is that she's
there !" a friend complained to me, not long
since. Everything has always been there, one
fancies. All one insists on is that neither Ann

Veronica nor Hilda Lessways is the normal representative of the sex. About the morality of Mr. Wells's and Mr. Bennett's books, there are probably a hundred opinions. One's own present quarrel with them is not that they are bad morals, but that they are bad biology.

TABU AND TEMPERAMENT

WHEN, I wonder, did the word "temperament" come into fashion with us? We can hardly have got it from the French, for the French mean by it something very different from what we do; though it is just possible that we did get it from them, and have merely Bowdlerized the term. At all events, whatever it stands for, it long since became a great social asset for women, and a great social excuse for men. Perhaps it came in when we discovered that artists were human beings. At least, for many years, we never praised an artist without using the word. It does not necessarily imply "charm," for people have charm irrespective of temperament, and temperament irrespective of charm. It is something that the Philistine never has: that we know. But what, by all the gods of clarity, does it mean?

It means, I fancy, in one degree or another, the personal revolt against convention. The individual who was "different," who did not let his inhibitions interfere with his epigrams, who was not afraid to express himself, who hated *clichés* of every kind—how well we know that figure in motley, who turned every occasion into a fancy-dress ball! All the inconvenient things he did were forgiven him, for the sake of the amusing things he said. Indeed, we hardly stopped to realize that his fascination was largely a matter of vocabulary. Now it is one thing to sow your wild oats in talk, and quite another to live by your own kaleidoscopic paradoxes. The people who frowned on the manifestations of "temperament" were merely those logical creatures who believed that if you expressed your opinions regardless of other people's feelings, you probably meant what you said. They did not know the pathology of epigram, the basic truth of which is that word-intoxicated people express an opinion long before they dream of holding it. They say what they think, whether they think it or not. Only, if you talk with incessant variety about what ought to be done, and then never do any of the wild things you recommend, you become in the end perfectly powerless as a foe of convention.

This tactical fact the unconventional folk have at last become aware of; and, accordingly, hostility to convention is ceasing somewhat to take itself out in phrases. Conventions, at the present moment, are really menaced. The most striking sign of this is that people are now making unconventionality a social virtue, instead of an unsocial vice. The switches have been opened, and the laden trains must take their chance of a destination.

The praise of temperament, I verily believe, was the entering wedge. But whatever the first cause, "conventional" is certainly in bad odor as an epithet. And this is really an interesting phenomenon, worth investigating. What is it that makes it a term of reproach? Why must you never say it about your dearest friend? Why must you contradict, in a shocked tone, if your dearest friend is said to be conventional? Most of my best friends are conventional, I am glad to say; but even I should never think of describing them to others thus.

Conventional people are supposed to lack intelligence—the power to think for themselves. (It seems to be pretty well taken for granted that you cannot think for yourself, and decide to think what the majority of your kind thinks. If you agree with the majority, it must be because you have no mental processes.) They are felt to lack charm: to have nothing unexpected and delightful to give you. And, nowadays, they are (paradoxes are popular) supposed to be perilous to society, because they are immovable, because they do not march with the times, because they cling to conservative conceptions while the parties of progress are re-making the world. All these reproaches are, at present, conveyed in the one word.

Now it is a great mistake to confound conventionality with simplicity—with that simplicity which indicates a brain inadequate to dealing with subtleties; or to confound "temperament" and unconventionality with a highly organized nature. The anthropologists have exploded all that. I have looked warily at anthropologists ever since the day when I went to hear a great Greek scholar lecture on the Iliad, and listened for an hour to talk about bull-roarers and leopard-societies. I doubt if the anthropologists have any more perspective than other scientists. I am as near being an old Augustan as any twentieth-century observer can be: "nihil humani," *etc.* But, for God's sake, let it be human! Palæontology is a poor substitute for history. No: I do not love any scientists, even the anthropologists. But I do think we ought to be grateful to them for proving to us that primitive people are a hundred times as conventional as we; and that their codes are almost too complicated for European minds to master. If any one is still under the dominance of Rousseau, Chateaubriand *et Cie.,* I wish he would sit down impartially before Messrs. Spencer and Gillen's exposition of group-marriage among the Australian aborigines. If, in three hours, he knows whom, supposing he were a Matthurie of the dingo totem, he could marry without incurring punishment, or even the death penalty, he had better take his subtlety into Central Australia: he is quite wasted on civilization.

Some one may retort that I am not exactly

making out a shining case for *tabu*, in citing the
very nasty natives of Australia as notable examples of what *tabu* can do for society. My
point is only this: that it is folly to chide conventional people for simplicity, since convention is a very complicated thing; or for dulness,
since it takes a good deal of intelligence and a
great many inhibitions to follow a social code.
To be different from everyone else, you have
only to shut your eyes and stop your ears, and
act as your nervous system dictates. By that
uncommonly easy means, you could cause a
tremendous sensation in any drawing-room,
while your brain went quite to sleep. The
natives of Central Australia are not nice; but
they are certainly nicer than they would be if
they practised free love all the year round,
instead of on rigidly specified occasions. Their
conventions are the only morality they have.
Some day, perhaps, they will do better. But it
will not be by forsaking conventions altogether.
For surely, in order to be attractive, we must
have some ideals, and above all some restraints.
Civilization is merely an advance in taste:
accepting, all the time, nicer things, and reject-
ing nasty ones.

When the temperamental and unconventional people are not mere plagiarists of dead
eccentrics, they lack, in almost every case, the
historic sense. I am far from saying that all
conventional folk have it; but they have at

least the merit of conforming. If they do not live by their own intelligence, it is because they live by something that they modestly value a good deal more. It is better that a dull person should follow the herd: his initiatives would probably be very painful to himself and every one else. No convention gets to be a convention at all except by grace of a lot of clever and powerful people first inventing it, and then imposing it on others. You can be pretty sure, if you are strictly conventional, that you are following genius—a long way off. And unless you are a genius yourself, that is a good thing to do. Unless we are geniuses, the lone hunt is not worth while: we had better hunt with the pack. Unless we are geniuses, there is much more fun in playing the game; there is much more fun in caste and class and clan. Unconventional people are apt to be Whistlers who cannot paint. Of course there is something very dull about the person who cannot give his reasons for his social creed. But if it is all a question of instinct, better a trained instinct than an untrained one. I am inclined to think that the mid-Victorian prejudice against—let us say—actors and actresses, was well founded. Under Victoria (or should one say under mid-Victoria?) stock companies were not chaperoned, and ladies and gentlemen went on the stage very infrequently. What is the point of admitting to your house some one who will be very uncomfortable there himself, and who will make every one else even more uncomfortable? It is not that we are afraid he will eat with his knife: that is a detail we might put up with. But eating or not eating with your knife is merely one of the little signs by which we infer other things. In this mad world, any one may do or be anything; but the man who has been brought up to eat with his knife is the less likely to have been brought up by people who would teach him to respect a woman or not to break a confidence. It is a stupid rule of thumb; but, after all, until you know a person intimately, how are you going to judge except by such fallible means? I have nothing in the world against Nature's noblemen; but the burden of proof is, of practical necessity, on their shoulders. Manners are not morals—precisely; yet, socially speaking, both have the same basis, namely, the Golden Rule. No one must be made more uncomfortable or more unhappy because he has been with you. Now, in spite of Oscar, it is worse to be unhappy than to be bored; and I would rather be the heroine of a not very clever comedy of manners than of a first-class tragedy. Most of us, when we are once over twenty, are no more histrionic, really, than that. The conventional person may bore you (though it is by no means certain that he will) but he will never, of his own volition, make you unhappy unless by way of justified retort. He will never put you, verbally or practically, into a nasty hole. Perhaps he will never give you the positive scarlet joys of shock and thrill. But, dear me! that brings us to another point. Conventional folk are often accused of being dull and valueless because they have no original opinions. (How we all love original opinions!) Well: very few people have any original opinions. Originality usually amounts only to plagiarizing something unfamiliar. "The wildest dreams of Kew are the facts of Khatmandhu"; and dead sages, if there were only retroactive copyrights, could sue most of our modern wits for their best things. What is even Jean-Jacques but Prometheus-and-water, if it comes to that? Very few people since Aristotle have said anything new. What passes for an original opinion is, generally, merely an original phrase. Old lamps for new—yes; but it is always the same oil in the lamp. Some people—like G. B. S. and Mr. Chesterton— seem to think that you can be original by contradicting other people—as if even the person who states a proposition did not know that you could make the verb negative if you chose! Often, they are so hard up that they have to contradict themselves. But they are supposed to be violently—subversively—enchantingly— original. Even the militant suffragettes have not "gone the whole hog": they have stopped

short of Aristophanes. What is the use of congratulating ourselves on our unprecedented
courage in packing the house solemnly for
Damaged Goods, when we have expurgated
the *Lysistrata*—and had the barest *succès
d'estime,* at that? No: our vaunted unconventionality is usually a matter of words. I have
tracked more than one delightful vocabulary
through the jungle, only to find that it brought
up at the literal inspiration of the Old Testament; and I have inwardly yawned away an
afternoon with a person who talked in *clichés,*
to discover perhaps, at twilight, that on some
point or other he was startlingly revolutionary.
The fact is that we are the soft prey of the
phrase; and the rhetoricians, whether we know
it or not, will always have their way with us.
Even the demagogue is only the rhetorician of
the gutter. "Take care of the sounds and the
sense will take care of itself"—as the Duchess
in *Alice* did *not* say. Dulness is a matter of
vocabulary; but there are no more dull people
among the conventional than among the unconventional. And if a person is to be unconventional, he must be amusing or he is intolerable:
for, in the nature of the case, he guarantees
you nothing but amusement. He does not guarantee you any of the little amenities by which
society has assured itself that, if it must go to
sleep, it will at least sleep in a comfortable
chair.

I was arguing at luncheon one day, with three clever women, the advantages and disadvantages of unconventionality. They were all perfectly conventional in a worldy sense, and perfectly convinced of the charms of unconventionality. (That is always the way: we sigh for the paradises that are not ours, like good Christians spurning the Apocalypse and coveting the Mohammedan heaven.) They cited to me a very amusing person—a priestess of intellectual revolt. Yes: she walked thirty blocks to lunch in a pouring rain, and when she came in she took off her wet hat, put it in her chair, and sat on it. The fact that my guest, did she choose, could afford to crown herself with pearls, would not make up to me for the consciousness that she was sitting on an oozing hat throughout luncheon. In spite of epigrams, I should feel, myself, perfectly wet through. Surely it is the essence of good manners not to make other people uncomfortable. Society, by its insisting on conventions, has merely insisted on certain convenient signs by which we may know that a man is considering, in daily life, the comfort of other people. No one except a reformer has a right to batten on other people's discomfort. And who would ever have wanted John Knox to dinner? To be sure, we are all a little by way of being reformers now—too much, I fear, as people went to see the same *Damaged Goods,* under shelter of

its sponsors, who cared for nothing whatever except being able to see a *risqué* play
without being looked at askance. But we shall
come to that aspect of it later.

Now "temperament," again, has often been
confused with charm; and conventional folk—
who are, by definition, dull and unoriginal, all
baked in the same archaic mould—are supposed to lack charm. They are at best like
inferior prints of a Hokusai from worn-out
blocks. The "justification" is bad. Their original may have been all very well; but they themselves are hopelessly *manqués,* and besides,
there are too many of them. How can they
have charm—that virtue of the individual,
unmatchable, unpredicable creature?

It is not against the acutest critics, the real
"collectors" and connoisseurs of human masterpieces, that I am inveighing. I am objecting
to the stupid criticisms of the stupid; to the
presence of "conventional" as a legitimate
curse on the lips of people who do not know
what they are talking about. One often hears
it—"I find him" (or "her") "so difficult to
talk to: he" (or "she") "is so conventional."
Good heavens! As if the conventional person
were not always at least easy to talk to! He
may be dull, but he knows his cues, and will
play the game as long as manners require. It
is the wild man on a rock, with a code that you
cannot be expected to know, because it is his

own peerless secret, who is hard to talk to. The people who say that conventional folk lack charm, often mean by "conventional" not wearing your heart on your sleeve. Now I positively like the sense, when I dine out, and stoop to rescue a falling handkerchief, that I am not going to rub my shoulder against a heart. What are hearts doing on sleeves? Am I a daw, that I should enjoy pecking at them? And who has any right to assume that, because they are not worn there, they are non-existent? It is of the essence of human nature to long for the unattainable. If you do not believe me, look at all the love-poetry in the world. As Mr. Chesterton says, "the coldness of Chloe" has been responsible for most of it. Certainly, if Chloe had worn her heart on her sleeve, the anthologies would have suffered. And with woman the case is the same. Let not the modern hero flatter himself that he will ever arouse the same kind of ardor in the female heart that the heroes of old did: those seared and saddened and magnificent creatures who bore hearts of flame within their granite breasts— but whose breasts were granite, all the same. No, gentlemen, women may marry you, but it is with a diminished thrill. We want—men and women both—to be intrigued; and I venture to say that for purposes of life, not of mere irresponsible conversation, it is the conventional person who intrigues us, since it is only the conventional person who creates the illusion of inaccessibility. He may be accessible, in reality; and the unconventional, temperamental person may be an impregnable fortress. That is the dizzy chance of life. But since all relations must have a beginning, the initial impression is the thing that counts. Of course one wants to know that the Queen of Spain has legs; but then we can be pretty sure that she has. We do not need a slit skirt to reassure us. One wants to know that there is a human face behind the mask; but who shall say that the mask does not heighten such beauty as there is? The conventional manner is a kind of domino: the accepted costume that all civilized people adopt for a time before unmasking. I do not suggest that we should disguise ourselves to the end; but that we should talk a little before we do unmask.

For there must be some ground on which to meet the person we do not know; and why may not the majority decide what grounds are the most convenient for all concerned? There must be some simplification of life: we cannot afford to have as many social codes as we have acquaintances. Imagine knowing five hundred people, and having to greet each with a different formula! Language would not run to it. And would it, in any case, constitute charm? Charm, as we all know, is a rare and treasurable thing; and no one can say where it will be found. But, as far as we can analyze it at all, its elements seem very likely to flourish in conventional air. Of course there may be a fearful joy in watching the man of whom you say: "One can never tell what he is going to do next." But you do not want him about, except on very special occasions. For the honest truth is that the unconventional person is almost never just unconventional enough. He is pretty sure to take you by surprise at some moment when you do not feel like being taken by surprise. Then you have to invent the proper way to meet the situation, which is a bore. It is not strange that some of our *révoltés* preach trial marriage: for the only safe way to marry them at all would be on trial. Until you had definitely experienced all the human situations with them, you would have no means of knowing how, in any given situation, they would behave. They might conform about evening-dress, and throw plates between courses; they might be charming to your friends, and ask the waiter to sit down and finish dinner with you. Or they might in all things, little and big, be irreproachable. The point is that you would never *know*. You could never take your ease in your inn, for nothing discoverable in earth or heaven would determine or indicate their code. Conventional manners are a kind of literacy test for the alien who comes among us. Not a fundamentally safe one? Perhaps not. But some test there must be; and this, on the whole, is the easiest to pass for those whom we are likely to want for intimates. That is really the social use of conventions.

And as for charm: your most charming people are those who constantly find new and unexpected ways of delighting us. Are such often to be found among people who are constantly finding new and unexpected ways of shocking us? I wonder. It seems to me doubtful, at the least. For shock—even the superficial social shock, the sensation that does not get far beneath the skin—is not delight. If you have ever really been shocked, you know that it is a disagreeable business. Of course, if some wonderful creature discovers the golden mean, the perfect note: to satisfy in all conventional ways, and still to be possessed of infinite variety in speech and mood—that wonderful creature is to be prized above the phœnix. But you cannot give rein to your own rich temperament in the matter, let us say, of auction bridge. The rules you invent as you go alone may be more shatteringly amusing than anything Hoyle ever thought of; but you cannot call it auction, and you must not expect other people to know how to return your leads. And usually it only means breaking rules without substituting anything better—revoking for a whim. Life is as co-operative a business as football; and we all know what becomes of the team of crack players when it faces a crack team. Only across the footlights are we apt to feel the charm of the Ibsen heroine; and even then we are apt to want supper and some irrelevant talk before we go to a dream-haunted couch. Now this matter of charm is not really an arguable one; for charm will win where it stands, whether it be conventional or unconventional. Every one knows about the young man who falls in love with the chorus-girl because she can kick his hat off, and his sister's friends can't or won't. But the youth who marries her, expecting that all her departures from convention will be as agile or as delightful to him as that, is still the classic example of folly. It is not senseless to bring marriage into the question, for when we advisedly call a man or a woman charming, we mean that that man or that woman would apparently be a good person with whom to form an intimate and lasting relation—not for us, ourselves, perhaps, but for some one else of our sort, in whom he or she contrives, by the alchemy of passion, to inspire the "sacred terror." To amuse for half an hour during which you incur no further responsibilities, to delight, in a relation which has no conceivable future, does not constitute charm; for it is of the essence of charm that it pulls the people who feel it—pulls, without ceasing. Charm magnetizes at long range. I contend only that conventional people are as

[149]

apt to have it as any one else, for they have the requisites, as far as requisites can be named.

As for the charm actually resident in conventionality *per se:* how should any one who does not feel it be converted to it by words of mine? For it is a beauty of form: not so much of good form as opposed to bad form, as of form opposed to formlessness. The foe of convention enters into the social plan, if at all, as a wild, Wagnerian *motif.* And the truly unconventional person has not even a *motif;* for he disdains repetition. He scorns to stand for anything whatever, and you are insulting his "temperament" if you suppose that it is capable of only one reaction on any given thing. The temperamental critic of literature—like Jules Lemaître in his salad days, before the Church had reclaimed him—prides himself on never thinking the same thing twice about any one masterpiece. Your temperamental creature will not twice hold the same opinion of any one person. If he has ever been notably pleased with a fellow-guest at dinner, it is safest never to repeat the combination. For the honor of his temperament, he must be disgusted the next time. It is his great gift not to be predicable, from day to day, from hour to hour. But a pattern is always predicable; and what you learn about a conventional person goes into the sum of knowledge: you do not have to unlearn it over night. Psychology becomes a lost art, a discredited science, when you deal with the temperamental person. You might as well have recourse to astrology. His very frankness is misleading. He can afford to give himself away, because he gives away nothing but the momentary mood. Never attempt to hold him to anything he has said: for his whole virtuosity consists in never saying the same thing twice, and never necessarily meaning it at all. He does very well for the idle hour, the box at the play; but for the business of life—oh!

And to some of us there is charm in the code itself—charm, that is, in any code, so long as it has behind it an idea, though an antique one, and is adhered to with faith. The right word must always seem "inevitable"; and so must, after all, the right act. An improvisation may be—must be, if it is to succeed—brilliant; but acts, like words, are best if they are in the grand style. Whether in speech or in manners, the grand style is never a mere magnificent idiosyncrasy; for the essence of the grand style is to carry with it the weight of the world.

And conventionality is now said to be subversive of the moral order! At least, most avowedly unconventional people are now treating themselves as reformers. Conventions did not fall, in spite of the neo-pagans; so the neo-Puritans must come in to make them totter. And with the neo-Puritans, it must be admitted (Cromwell did not live in vain) most of the

charm of unconventionality has gone. It has
become a brutal business. The neo-pagans realized that, to be endured at all, they must make
us smile. If they told a *risqué* story, it must be
a really funny one. At the present moment, we
may not go in for *risqué* remarks in the interests of humor, but we may make them in the
interests of morality. We may say anything we
like at a dinner-party, so long as we put no wit
into saying it. We must not quote eighteenth-
century *mots*, but we may discuss prostitution
with some one we have never seen before. Anything is forgiven us, so long as we are not
amusing. If we only draw long faces, we may
even descend to anecdote. And when people
are asked to break with conventions in the
interests of morality, they may feel that they
have to do it. It has always been permitted to
make the individual uncomfortable for the
good of the community. So we cannot snub the
philanthropists as we would once have snubbed
the underbred: for thereby we somehow damn
ourselves. If you refuse to discuss the white
slave traffic, you are guilty of civic indifference;
and that is the one form of immorality for
which now there is no sympathy going. I may
have no ideas and no information about the
white slave traffic, but I ought to be interested
in it—interested to the point of hearing the
ideas, and gathering the information, of the
person whom I have never seen before. It is
the "Shakespeare and the musical glasses" of

the present day. Vain to take refuge in plays or books: for what play or book is well known at all unless it deals with the social evil?

Now it has already been pointed out that vice commission reports have done as much harm as good. The discussion of them is not limited to the immune, "highbrow" caste. I know of one quite unimperilled stenographer who was frightened by them into the psychopathic ward at Bellevue; and we have all read instructive comments in the daily papers which reiterate that virtue is ten dollars a week. A much lower figure than Becky Sharp's, but the principle is the same. Out of her weekly wage, we may be sure the shopgirl (it is always the shopgirl!) buys the paper—and therewith her Indulgence for future faults, much cheaper than Tetzel ever sold one. For Purgatory now is replaced by Public Opinion. Even my own small town is not free from the prophylactic "movie." One small boy nudges another, as they pass the placarded entrance, exclaiming debonairly, "Oh, this 'ere white slave tramc, y'know!" And the child, I have been given to understand, is the father of the man. The unconventional reformers quote to themselves, I suppose:

> Vice is a monster of such frightful mien, *etc.*

It never occurs to them to finish the sentence:

> We first endure, then pity, then embrace.

The fact is that Anglo-Saxon society has got beyond the enduring stage, and is largely occupied in pitying. There is a general sense that the people at large, in all moral matters, know better than the specialists. We will take our creed not from the theologians, but from Mr. Winston Churchill; and we will take our pathology not from medical treatises, but from Brieux. We will discuss the underworld at dinner because, between the fish and the entrée, the thin lady with the pearls may say something valuable about it. If we are made uncomfortable by the discussion, it only shows that we are selfish pigs.

Now I see no reason why decent-minded people should not discuss with their intimate friends anything they please. If you are really intimate with any one, you are not likely to discuss things unless you both please. But I do see, still, a beautiful result of the old order that the new order does not tend to produce. The conventional avoidance as a general subject of conversation of sex in all its phases was a safeguard to sensibilities. You cannot, in one sense, discuss sex quite impersonally, for every one is of one sex or the other. The people who cry out against the segregation of the negro in government offices have hardly realized that non-segregation is objected to, not because of itself, but because of miscegenation. There is a little logic left in the world; and there are some people who perceive that sequence, whether they phrase it or not. Social distinctions concern themselves ultimately with whom you may and whom you may not marry. You do not bring people together in society who are *tabu* to each other. Not that you necessarily expect, out of a hundred dinner-parties, any one marriage to result; but you assume social equality in the people seated about your board. Is not, in the last analysis, the only sense in such a phrase as "social equality," the sense of marriageability? Even conventions are not so superficial as they seem; and they have that perfectly good human basis. It is vitally important to the welfare and the continuance of the civilized race that sex-sensibilities should be preserved. Otherwise you will not get the romantic mating; and the unromantic mating, once well established in society, will give rise to a perfectly transmissible (whether by heredity or environment, O shade of Mendel!) brutality. It is brutalizing to talk promiscuously of things that are essentially private to the individual; just as it is brutalizing (I believe no one questions that) for a family and eight boarders to sleep in one room—even a large room. All violations of essential privacy are brutalizing. We do not take our toothbrushes with us when we go out to dinner, and if we did, and did not mind (very soon we should not), the practice, I am sure, would

[155]

have a brutalizing effect. A certain amount of plain speaking is, perhaps, a good thing; but there is no doubt that at present we have far too much of it to suit most of us, and I cannot see why we should be made to endure it just because a few people who are by way of calling themselves moralists cannot get on with society on its own terms.

It has long been a convention among people who are not cynical that bodily matters are not spoken of in mixed and unfamiliar gatherings. Of course, our great-grandmothers were prudes. The reason why they talked so much about their souls, I fancy, is that there was hardly a limb or a feature of the human body that they thought it proper to mention. They were driven back on religion because they held that the soul really had nothing to do with the body at all. The psychiatrists have done their best to take away from us that (on the whole) comforting belief. In America, at least, we are finding it harder and harder to get out of the laboratory. It is the serious and patriotic American in *The Madras House* who asks the astonished Huxtable, "But are you the mean sensual man?" In *The Madras House* the question is screamingly funny; but I cannot imagine any man's liking, in his own house, to have the question put to him by a total stranger. The fact is that we have dragged our Ibsen and our Strindberg and our Sudermann lovingly across the footlights, and are hugging them to our hearts in the privacy of our boxes. We have decided that manners shall consist entirely of morals. It is just possible that, in the days when morals consisted largely of manners, fewer people were contaminated. You cannot shock a person practically whom you are totally unwilling to shock verbally; and if you are perfectly willing to shock an individual verbally, the next thing you will be doing is to shock him practically. Above all, when we become incapable of the shock verbal, there will be nothing left for the unconventional people but the shock practical. And that, I imagine, is what we are coming to—all in the interests of morality, be it understood. At no time in history, perhaps, have the people who are not fit for society had such a glorious opportunity to pretend that society is not fit for them. Knowledge of the slums is at present a passport to society — so much the parlor philanthropists have achieved — and all they have to do is to prove that they know their subject. It is an odd qualification to have pitched on; but gentlemen and ladies are always credulous, especially if you tell them that they are not doing their duty.

Moreover, when you make it a moral necessity for the young to dabble in all the subjects that the books on the top shelf are written about, you kill two very large birds with one stone: you satisfy precocious curiosities, and

you make them believe that they know as much
about life as people who really know something. If college boys are solemnly advised to
listen to lectures on prostitution, they will listen; and who is to blame if some time, in a less
moral moment, they profit by their information? If we discuss the pathology of divorce
with the first-comer, what is to prevent divorce
from becoming, in the end, as natural as daily
bread? And if nothing is to be *tabu* in talk,
how many things will remain *tabu* in practice?
The human race is, in the end, as relentlessly
logical as that. Even the aborigines that we
have occasionally mentioned turn scandals over
to the medicine-man, and keep a few delicate
silences themselves. Perhaps we are "returning
to Nature," as the Rousseauists wanted us to;
with characteristic Anglo-Saxon thoroughness,
going the savages one better. But it is a pity to
forget how to blush; for though in the ideal
society a blush would never be forced to a
cheek, it would not be because nothing was considered (as a German might say) blushworthy.
Each man's private conscience ought to be a
nice little self-registering thermometer: he
ought to carry his moral code incorruptibly and
explicitly within himself, and not care what the
world thinks. The mass of human beings, however, are not made that way; and many people
have been saved from crime or sin by the simple
dislike of doing things they would not like to

confess to people with a code. I do not contend that that is a high form of morality; but it has certainly saved society a good many practical unpleasantnesses. And we are clearly courting the danger of essentially undiscussable actions when we admit every action to discussion.

I saw it seriously contended in some journal or other, not long ago, that, whether any other women were enfranchised or not, prostitutes ought undoubtedly to have the vote, because only thus could the social evil be effectively dealt with. Incredible enough; but there it was. Not many people, perhaps, would agree with that particular reformer; but undoubtedly there is a mania at present, in the classes that used to be conventional, for getting one's information from the other camp. It is valuable to know the prostitute's opinion — facts never come amiss; but why assume that we have only to know it to hold it? Is it not conceivable that other generations than our own have known her opinions, and that lines of demarcation have been drawn because a lot of people, as intelligent as we, did not agree with her? The present tendency, however, is to consider every one's opinion important, in social and ethical matters, except that of respectable folk. My own pessimistic notion is, as I have hinted, that the philanthropic assault on the conventional code has come primarily from people who were too ignorant, or too lazy, or too

undisciplined, to submit to the code; and that
the success of the assault results from the sheer
defenceless niceness—the mingled altruism and
humility—of the people accused of conventionality. At all events, the fact is that our
reticences have somehow become cases of cowardice, and our rejections forms of brutality.
We are all a little pathetic in our credulity, and
we are very like Moses Primrose at the fair.
Well: let us buy green spectacles if we must;
but let us, as long as we can, refuse to look
through them!

It may seem a far cry from "temperament"
to social service. I have known a great many
people who went in for social service, and I do
not think it is. The motives of the heterogeneous foes of convention may lie as far apart
as the Poles (one Pole is very like the other,
by the way, as far as we can make out from
Peary and Amundsen) but the object is the
same: to destroy the complicated fabric which
the centuries have lovingly built up. (Even if
you call it "restoration," it is apt to amount to
the same thing, as any good architect knows.)
At the bar of Heaven, sober Roundheads and
drunken rioters will probably be differently
dealt with; but here on earth, both have
been given to smashing stained-glass windows.
Many of us do not believe in capital punishment, because thus society takes from a man
what society cannot give. The iconoclasts do

the same thing; for civilization, whether it be perfect or not, is a fruit of time. Conventions are easy to come by, if you are willing to take conventions like those of the Central Australians. The difference between a perfected and a barbaric convention is a difference of refinement, in the old alchemical sense. A lot of the *tabu* business is too stupid and meaningless for words. Civilization has been a weeding-out process, controlled and directed by increasing knowledge. We have infinitely more conventions than the aborigines: we simply have not such silly ones. The foes of modern convention are not suggesting anything wiser, or better, or more subtle: they are only attacking all convention blindly, as if the very notion of *tabu* were wrong. The very notion of *tabu* is one of the rightest notions in the world. Better any old *tabu* than none, for a man cannot be said to be "on the side of the stars" at all, unless he makes refusals. What the foes of convention want is to have all *tabu* overthrown. It is very dull of them, for even if a cataclysm came and helped them out—even if we were all turned, over night, into potential fossils for the delight of future scientists — the next beginnings of society would be founded on *tabu*. We shudder at the Central Australians; we should hate life on their terms. But I would rather live among the Warramunga than among the twentieth-century anarchists, for I cannot conceive a

more odious society than one where nothing is
considered indecent or impious. We may think
that the mental agility of the Warramunga
could be better applied. Well: in time, it will
be. But they are lifted above the brute just in
so far as they develop mental agility in the
framing of a moral law, however absurd a one.
I said that their conventions were almost too
complicated for us to master. That, I fancy, is
because any mind they have, they give to their
conventions. It is the natural consequence of
giving your mind to science and history and
philology and art, that you simplify where you
can; also, that your conventions become puri-
fied by knowledge. Even the iconoclasts of the
present day do not want us to throw away such
text-book learning as we have achieved. They
do ask us, though, to throw away the racial
inhibitions that we have been so long acquiring.
Is it possible that they do not realize what a
slow and difficult business it is to get any particular opinion into the instincts of a race? Only
the "evolution" they are so fond of talking
about can do that. Perhaps we ought to take
comfort from the reflection. But it is easier to
destroy than to build up; and they are quite
capable of wasting a few thousand years of
our time.

No: the iconoclasts want to bring us, if possible, lower than the Warramunga. Some of
them might be shocked at the allegation, for

some of them, no doubt, are idealists—after the fashion of Jean-Jacques, be it understood. These are merely, one may say respectfully, mistaken: for they do not reckon with human nature any more than do the socialists. But the majority, I incline to believe, are merely the natural foes of dignity, of spiritual hierarchy, of wisdom perceived and followed. They object to guarded speech and action, because they themselves find self-control a nuisance. So, often, it is; but if the moral experience of mankind has taught us anything, it has taught us that, without self-control, you get no decent society at all. When the mistress of Lowood School told Mr. Brocklehurst that the girls' hair curled naturally, he retorted: "Yes, but we are not to conform to nature; I wish these girls to become children of grace." We do not sympathize with Mr. Brocklehurst's choice of what was to be objected to in nature; we do not, indeed, sympathize with him in any way, for he was a hypocrite. But none the less, it is better to be, in the right sense, a child of grace than a child of nature. Attila did not think so; and Attila sacked Rome. We may be sacked—the planet is used to these *débâcles*—but let us not, either as a matter of mistaken humility or by way of low strategy, pretend that the Huns were Crusaders!

THE BOUNDARIES OF TRUTH

IT is pretty much taken for granted by decent folk that the truth should be told in all circumstances. "It is never permissible to lie" has been, ever since the Christian era came in, the common opinion, if not the common practice. And yet, which one of us has never lied, I will not say against his conscience, but for the very sake of his conscience? Conventional religion has been assumed to be our sole guide, while our actual conduct is usually based on the different, and more explicit, code of honor. Honor is not religion, though with real religion it has always been at peace; civilized manners are not religion, though, again, they have always been at peace with it. In the matter of lying, both honor and civilized manners have a great deal to say; and the fact that we realize this subconsciously is responsible for a great many minor perplexities.

Strictly speaking, in Candide's "best of possible worlds" lies should not pass human lips. There are many people who stick to the literal interpretation of the precept: ladies, for example, who retire to the back porch before they permit their maids to tell the unwelcome caller that they are "out." There, presumably, they gaze at the blue sky, and congratulate themselves on their unimpeachable veracity. Yet even scrupulous people allow their servants to say they are out when they are in, because "out" is conventionally understood to mean many things. On the other hand, Mr. Chesterton tells us that, under certain conditions, mere silence is the most damnable lie of all. The matter is not so simple as it seems: its intricacies may become a morass for the unwary, and an enchanted garden for the casuist.

Very few people, I fancy, would say, after deliberation, that no lie was ever justified. To be sure, I once heard a serious young man protest that Shakespeare had damned Desdemona by allowing her, at her last gasp, to exculpate Othello. I have also known people who objected vehemently to the late Mark Twain because he said so many things that were not so. But there are occasions when lies are taken for granted, even by the law. A man on trial for his life is supposed to tell the truth, but not if it will incriminate him. A wife is not dragged to the witness-stand against her will to testify against her husband — no one would legitimately expect anything but perjury from her. I do not see much difference between legally permitting a man to say "Not guilty" when he is guilty, and legally permitting him to lie. Is there any solitary maiden lady who would not willingly give the midnight marauder to under-

stand that her husband was just coming down
the stairs, armed to the teeth? A man is not
supposed, except by an extinct type of Puritan,
to "give away" the lady who has made sacrifices for him; and even the extinct type of
Puritan would hardly expect you to tell your
hostess that her dinner-party had been dull.
From this heterogeneous group of examples,
one may infer that there are lies and lies; and
while it is never permissible to lie, it is sometimes quite unpermissible to do anything else.

Most lies of the decenter sort are social.
"The admixture of a lie doth ever give pleasure," said the moralist Bacon. There is certainly very little defence for the lie that does
not give pleasure. It is to save other people's
feelings, not our own, that we tell lies. Let me
put a case quite bluntly. How, without lying, is
a man to thank his small niece properly for the
necktie which she has selected for his Christmas present? No one wants merely to be
thanked for one's trouble; every one wants to
be told that his taste has been perfect. Now
that the late Phillips Brooks's handsome eva-
sion of fact has become historic, who ever
dares *not* to praise a baby explicitly? I confess
that it goes against the grain with me to say
that I have enjoyed something which I have
detested; and I have frequently accepted invitations (especially over the telephone) because
my tongue would not twist itself round the
phrase "another engagement" when the other

engagement was non-existent. But I have never had the slightest compunction about saying that I was sorry I had another engagement, when I did have another engagement and was not sorry.

I know only one person whom I could count on not to indulge herself in these conventional falsehoods, and she has never been able, so far as I know, to keep a friend. The habit of literal truth-telling, frankly, is self-indulgence of the worst. Nothing could be more delightful, in an evil sense, than telling certain people that their Christmas presents, their babies, and their hospitalities are all horrors which defy description; especially if one could count it a virtue to one's self to say those things starkly. But one cannot keep that weapon only for one's foes: the only excuse for saying inexcusable things is that one always says them. Roughly speaking, one's friends are the people of whom one thinks, habitually, pleasant things. But even friends can be annoying, or unbeautiful, or dull. And it is of the essence of those manners which are morals not to tell them so if one can help it. "Faithful are the wounds of a friend"— and must sometimes be dealt. But no stabbing over non-essentials! And above all, no stabbing when it is a pleasure to stab. Sometimes these truth-tellers congratulate themselves that their praise is immensely enhanced by its rarity. There, I fancy, they are mistaken: for in the first place, praise that is too long on the way

loses its savor; and in the second, they acquire,
I have noticed, a censorious habit of mind that
prevents them from praising at all.

No: in the course of mere conventional living, a certain amount of lying must be done.
"How do you do?" "I am very well, thank
you." You may have indigestion, and in that
case you have lied. Yet is it your business to
make your acquaintance uncomfortable by telling him the facts in the case? Certain things
are true of any man personally which have
nothing to do with his social existence: personally, if he has a toothache, he has it; socially,
he has not a toothache unless he mentions it.
Then, there are lies which are not verbal at
all — lies of implication. The early Puritans
who objected to paint and powder, objected to
them, I fancy, on perfectly Catholic grounds—
it was immoral to make yourself attractive,
and paint and powder were literally meretri-
cious. On the same principle, to this day, a nun
cuts off her hair. The modern feeling against
paint and powder—for it does in some quarters survive—is rather, I imagine, on the score
of dishonesty. You are not supposed to disguise
a beautiful complexion if you really have it.
But if you have not a good complexion, you are
deceiving people — you are acting a lie — by
making yourself look as if you had. The ground
of the objection has shifted.

Some author—is it Mr. Kipling?—says of

one of his heroines that she was as honest as her own front teeth. I know a great many people who are as honest as their own front teeth are false; and certainly no one expects them to go about calling attention to the skill of their dentist. Perhaps some sophist will say that between wearing false hair and declaring one's false hair to be one's own, there is all the difference in the world. I protest that it is tacit falsehood to wear it at all—unless one does it after the fashionless fashion of an ancient lady I knew in my childhood who, quite bald at the age of ninety-five, hung two wads of chestnut hair across her head, like saddle-bags, on a black velvet ribbon. And such tacit falsehoods are all in the spirit of the conventional politeness we use daily. To rouge a pale face may be vanity; but to thank a stupid hostess for the pleasure she has not given, is loving one's neighbor as one's self. I am inclined to think that even rouge is more often than not altruistic in intention. One does not wish, for the sake of society, to be either a fright or a brute. Certain things are demanded of every man who meets the world on its own ground. From the moment he has "accepted with pleasure," he has agreed to play the game; and it is as unfair of him to give or take the wrong cues as it would be for the castle to insist on making the knight's move. No: we need not go out of our way to lie; but we must not, even to be clever, tell the truth when an innocent lie is innocently demanded of us.

It occurs to me that my examples of conventional falsehood are largely feminine. So, I fancy, they should be. One of the reasons, surely, why women have been credited with less perfect veracity than men is that the burden of conventional falsehood falls chiefly on them. A man expects his wife to do this kind of thing for him. It is she who accepts or refuses their common invitations, directs their joint social manœuvres, encounters the world for them both on the purely social side. He is not expected to do it any more than he is expected to order the dinner. There is more straight-from-the-shoulder talk, I imagine, among men by themselves than among women by themselves; but that is partly because women slip out of the social harness less frequently and less easily. A man among men is perhaps (I speak under correction) more inveterately his personal self; a woman among women more inveterately her social self. It may be that it is easier to wear the harness constantly than to gall one's shoulders afresh each day with putting it on. I am inclined to think that women are as honest with their intimate friends as are men; but—they have had an age-long training in the penalties of making one's self unpleasant. So many low motives are imputed to women—and most of them, at the present day, quite unjustly

—that they are driven to the lesser mendacities for the sake of getting some justice done them. When Mr. A. asks Mrs. B. if she does not think Mrs. C. beautiful, she is almost bound to say that she does, though she does not. Otherwise, she will be taken for a jealous fool. One lie is better than two; and it is better to be thought a fool when you are not, than jealous and a fool when you are neither. Comparatively few people, however, will cavil at these mendacities, which are indeed ψευδῆ ἀψευδῆ — as mechanical and uncalculated as a gentleman's "I beg your pardon" when a lady has insisted on colliding with him in the street. Truth is not so difficult to bound on that side; for most people recognize the social exigency, and if you are praising some one's unskilful cook on one day, the chances are that she will be congratulating you on your amateur gardening the next. We simply have to be polite, as our race and clime understand politeness; and no one except a *naïf* is really going to take this sort of thing seriously. It is perhaps regrettable that we do not carry courtesy even further; for nothing makes people so worthy of compliments as occasionally receiving them. One is more delightful for being told one is delightful—just as one is more angry for being told one is angry. Let us pass, however, to more debatable ground.

There is an old refrain which runs, "Ask me

no questions, I'll tell you no lies." I am inclined
to think that it is full of social philosophy.
Most of us, probably, have put up our hardest
fights for veracity on occasions when questions
have been asked us that never should have
been asked. "Refuse to answer," says the ghost
of that extinct Puritan whom we have evoked.
An absurd counsel: for, as we all know, to
most of these questions no answer is the most
explicit answer of all. If the Devil has given
you wit enough, you may contrive to keep the
letter of the commandment. But usually that
does not happen. I dare say many moralists
will not agree with me; but I hold that a question put by some one who has no right,
from any point of view, to the information
demanded, deserves no truth. If a casual gos-
sip should ask me whether my unmarried great-
aunt lived beyond her means, I should feel
justified in saying that she did not, although it
might be the private family scandal that she
did. There are inquiries which are a sort of
moral burglary. The indiscreet questioner—
and by indiscreet questions I mean questions
which it is not conceivably a man's duty either
to the community or to any individual to answer
—is a marauder, and there is every excuse for
treating him as such. I am sure that every
reader remembers, in his own experience, such
questions, and counts among his acquaintance at
least one such questioner. Let him say whether,

in these conditions, he has felt it his moral duty
to hand over information, any more than he
would consider it his moral duty to hand over
his plate to a thief. I am not speaking of cases
where the temptation to lie is merely the temptation to save one's face: it is not permissible to
lie merely to save one's face. But it is sometimes
permissible to lie to save another person's face
—as it was pardonable, surely, in Desdemona
to declare that Othello had not murdered her.

In regard to the lie of exaggeration, a word
should perhaps parenthetically be said. We all
know the child who has seen two elephants in
the garden eating the roses. We also know the
delightful grown-up who "embroiders" his nar-
ratives. He will never tell the same adventure
twice with the same details. The fact remains
that he may each time leave you with precisely
the same impression of the adventure in its
entirety. It is quite possible that you trust him
exceedingly. Of course it is also possible that
his *ben trovato* is never *vero*. You will have
to determine after long experience of him
whether he is fundamentally false, or merely
has a sense of style. Personally, I know exag-
gerators of both kinds: people whose lies are
only picturesque adjectives, and people whose
picturesque adjectives are only lies. There is
a subtle distinction between the two. At the
risk of being at loggerheads with the rhetoricians, one must say that truth goes deeper than

words, and that there is not much in a truthful-
ness which is only phrase-deep.

The old ladies who are shivering on the back
porch will disapprove of me for saying these
things, almost as much as I disapprove of them
for being on the back porch. To speak frankly,
I have not found that the people who cling to
the letter are always the people who cling to
the spirit of the law. Some of the men and
women who will not say in so many words the
thing which is not, will deliberately give a false
impression. They are not the servants of truth;
they are the parasites of truth. The ladies I
have referred to may be technically "out"; but
they are really "out" only to the undesired visi-
tor—exactly as much as if they had stopped in
their own sitting-rooms. (Remember, please,
that I am not speaking of the people who receive the unwelcome caller rather than permit
a maid to fib—they are in a very different
case.) I should not instinctively go to these
people for an accurate account of a serious situation. Any one whose conscience is satisfied
with that kind of loyalty to fact knows very
little about the spirit of truth.

I do not jeer at literal accuracy: I think it
an excellent safeguard for all of us. The person
who has never indulged in a literal falsehood
is the less likely to have indulged in a real
one. Generally speaking, words follow facts
with a certain closeness. Not always, however.

I may truthfully say that my teeth are my own, if I have paid for them; but I shall none the less give a wrong impression to the engaging creature who has asked me if they are false. Substitute serious equivalents for that kind of veracious reply, and you will see what I mean. I am not at all sure that, where there is room for doubt, the people I have cited will not largely take the benefit of the doubt to themselves. I am not sure, for example, that the formula "I will not tell any one" stands to them for anything but a fallible human prophecy—something apt to be set at naught by the God who maketh diviners mad. I strongly suspect that mere loyalty will never make them hold their tongues. And I am quite sure that they will often be silent when silence is the most damnable lie of all. For, in their technical sense, silence can never be a lie.

In this short distance, we have come near to the heart of the matter. Remember that the only lie forbidden in the Decalogue is false witness against one's neighbor. I may feel real respect for the lady on the porch—when I think that it may be hailing, I feel positive awe—but I should not like to make her the recipient of an intimate confidence. Such a person is wholly at the mercy of the unscrupulous. To be, for one's self, at the mercy of the unscrupulous, suggests, I admit, the saint; to be, for one's friends, at the mercy of the unscrupulous, suggests the cad. It is not, for the normal person, a pleasant thing to lie: it is much easier to record the truth quite automatically. There is in each of us who have been decently brought up a natural antipathy to saying "the thing which is not." The basis of truth is so much the finest basis on which to meet one's fellow-men! I have much sympathy with the unpopular people who cannot bring themselves, even in a ball-room, to "play the game." Of all ugly things to be, perhaps a liar is the ugliest. And yet, and yet— We may not go into Victor Hugo's rapture over the nun in *Les Misérables* who gave the mendacious answer to Javert; but which of us wishes she had told the inspector that Jean Valjean was actually in the room? Fortunately, such crucial instances are rare; and usually we can benefit our friends most by telling the truth about them—if it were not so, they would not be beloved. It is a poor cause which has to be lied for regularly. But in the rare case like that of Sœur Simplice, let us hope that we, too, should lie, and be as sure as she of making our peace with Heaven.

For one's self alone, it is a question whether any lie could bring such luxury as that of telling the simple truth. To lie to save one's self is the mark of the beast; to lie to save another person may make one distrust the cosmos, but at least it is a purer fault. For it seems to be agreed on by all codes that the unselfish motive is a mightily purging element. On the whole, I should say that the person who likes to lie should never, in any circumstances, be allowed to. Leave the lying to the people who hate it. You will not find them indulging often.

Perhaps the greatest conflict for Puritan youth has always come when it faced for the first time the unfamiliar shape of Honor. Honor and John Calvin have fought on many a strange battlefield for the young soul, and the young soul must often have wondered which was friend and which was foe.

> Honour and wit, foredamned they sit,

sings Kipling in an atavistic moment. Which of us has not at some time or other shudderingly understood him? And yet it is only the fortuitous trappings of Honor which can so disturb. For the truest thing about Honor is that, like Charity, it "seeks not itself"; and Honor in the mediæval sense was the darling child of the Church. Honor does not break its word; it protects the weak against itself, and against others; it keeps its engagements. It is more immediately concerned with its duty to humanity than with its duty to God; which is doubtless why the Puritan mystic saw it as a foe. The code of honor is the etiquette-book of the Christian; and the people who have attacked it are the people who have considered that Christians needed no etiquette. By our ancestors who were bred in the cold and windy times of the Reformation it was held to deal chiefly with duelling, gaming, and illicit affairs. "The debt of honor," "the affair of honor"—what do even these corrupted phrases mean except that the gentleman has found more ways to bind himself than the laws of the land afford? I do not know that Honor ever compelled a man to gamble or to provoke a quarrel; but if he has gambled or if he has quarrelled—if he has undertaken to play the lamentable game —he must not skulk behind a policeman, like a cry-baby or a *sans-culotte,* because things have not gone his way. If he has broken, he must pay.

Part of the code of honor begins only when the Christian precept has been broken. Is it so bad a thing, in a fallible world, to be told what to do after you have once done something wrong? The Catechism, as a practical guide, is wofully incomplete without the code of the gentleman as an appendix. If you had sinned, the Puritan told you to repent; and he was quite right. But there is work left for the sinner after the repenting has been done. Both Honor and the Catechism will do their best to keep you out of a mess. The difference comes later: for after you have got into a mess, the Catechism leaves you to God, while Honor shows you how, if you have done ill to fellow beings, to repair that ill and not extend it.

Honor is a matter of practical politics—

frightfully unpractical politics, in another sense, they often are. A cynical young woman once said to me that she found cads more interesting than gentlemen, because you could always tell what a gentleman would do in a given situation, whereas you could never tell, in any situation, what a cad would do. Cads may or may not be the proper sport of cynical young women; but to the average busy creature the gentleman is wholly delightful in that he is wholly predicable. The Christian is not predicable, for the simple reason that he has been given a counsel of perfection. You know that any given Christian will, by the day of his majority, have done some, at least, of the things which the Catechism has expressly warned him not to do. "The way that can be walked upon is not the perfect way," said Laotse long ago. The Church does not believe that you have always done everything that your sponsors in baptism so cheerfully said you would do. The confessional is itself the greatest confession that the Church has ever made. One of the most convenient things about Honor is that its explicit code is limited; and you can say of some men when they die that they have never for a moment ceased to be gentlemen. Honor is of the world, worldly—and some people have distorted that magnificent fact into an accusation. That is what Mr. Kipling has done in "Tomlinson."

All this about Honor is not so much a digres-

sion as an approach. For if few people will
quarrel with the lies of implication and of convention, and most people pray to be delivered
from the lie of self-defence, the lie "of obligation" cannot be juggled away; and it is the lie
of obligation which Honor commands. Honor
has never permitted, still less commanded, a lie
for personal gain or satisfaction of any kind;
but there are cases when the gentleman must
lie if he is to be a gentleman. The gentleman
does not betray the friend who has trusted him,
even though he may bitterly object to having
that friend's secrets on his hands. From that
supreme obligation lies sometimes of necessity
result. I said just now that Honor and John
Calvin must often have fought for the young
soul; and it does not take an over-vivid imagination to conceive cases. Religion (in spite of
the Decalogue) has tended to lump all lies
together as the offspring of the Devil, while
the code of the gentleman has always set aside
a few lies as consecrated and *de rigueur*. But
the gentleman, I venture to say, has always
told those lies in the spirit in which a man lays
down his life for his friend. For no gentleman
lies, on any occasion, with unmixed pleasure.
He feels, rather, as if he had put on rags.

It is easier—as some sociologists do—to
plot the curves of a desire than to fix the
boundaries of truth. The domain of truth is
not world-wide: that, we know. They must be

home-keepers indeed — perpetually cradled — who need never lie. Literal truth is imprisoned in a palace, like the Pope in the Vatican, affecting to be the ruler of the world. Even the faithful know that the claim is vain. The lies of obligation and convention are not, in the deepest sense, unveracious; for they are not preeminently intended to deceive. We expect them of other civilized beings and expect other civilized beings to expect them of us. Speaking such falsehoods, and such falsehoods only, we are still on truth's own ground. The lie told for the liar's own sake marks the moment when a man has passed from beneath her standard, across her shadowy sphere of influence, and is already hot-foot into the jungle.

MISS ALCOTT'S NEW ENGLAND

I REMEMBER being very much impressed
—and not a little shocked—when a friend
of mine told me that she had never, in her
childhood, been able to get any real pleasure
out of Louisa Alcott's stories. It had never
occurred to me that being brought up in New
York instead of in New England, or even
being of Southern instead of Pilgrim stock,
could make all that difference. Miss Alcott
seemed the safe inheritance, the absolutely inevitable delight, of childhood. *Little Women*
was as universal as *Hamlet*. I remembered
perfectly that French playmates of mine in
Paris had loved *Les Quatre Filles du Doc-
teur March* (though the French version was
probably somewhat expurgated). If children
of a Latin—moreover, of a Royalist and Catholic — tradition could find no flaw in Miss
Alcott's presentment of young life, I could not
see why any free-born American child should
fail to find it sympathetic.

I questioned my friend more closely. Her
answer set me thinking; and it is probably to
her that I owe my later appreciation of Miss
Alcott's special quality and special documen-
tary value. For what my friend said was simply

that the people in the books were too underbred for her to get any pleasure out of reading
about them. My friend was not, when I knew
her, a snob; and I took it that she had made
the criticism originally at a much earlier age.
All children are as snobbish as they know how
to be; and I fancy that the child's perennial
delight in fairy-tales is not due solely to the
epic instinct. One is interested in princes and
princesses, when one is eight, simply because
they are princes and princesses. Of royalty, one
is perfectly sure. I have never known a child
who did not prefer the goose-girl to be a princess in disguise, or who felt any real sympathy
with the princess who was only a disguised
goose-girl. You do not have to expound the
Divine Right to any one under twelve. Peas-
ants are an acquired taste; and socialism is an
illusion of age.

Out of such axioms as these, I made my
explanation of my friend's heterodoxy. I remembered my own reaction, when very young,
on a story that centred in a masked ball to
which all the inhabitants of the kingdom were
bidden. All the milkmaids went as court ladies,
and all the court ladies went as milkmaids—a
mere rounding out of the Petit Trianon episode. The moral was obvious; and I recall
being frightfully disturbed by my own absolute
certainty that, if I had been going to a masked
ball, I should, without hesitation, have gone as

grandly as I possibly could. I should never have gone as a milkmaid, so long as the costumer had a court train left. Did it perhaps mean that I was, on the whole, nearer to the milkmaid than to the court lady? I did not like the story, but I have never, to this day, forgotten it. Perhaps my friend had been of the same age when she discriminated against Miss Alcott. But then, I and my contemporaries had made no such discrimination. As I say, it set me to thinking. Since then, I have read Miss Alcott over, not once, but many times, and I think I understand.

The astounding result of re-reading Miss Alcott at a mature age is a conviction that she probably gives a better impression of mid-century New England than any of the more laborious reconstructions, either in fiction or in essay. The youth of her characters does not hinder her in this; for childhood, supremely, takes life ready-made. Mr. Howells's range is wider, and he is at once more serious and more detached. Technically, he and Miss Alcott can be compared as little as *Madame Bovary* and the *Bibliothèque Rose*. Yet, although their testimonies often agree, his world does not "compose" as hers does. It may be his very realism—his wealth of differentiating detail, his fidelity to the passing moment—that makes his early descriptions of New England so out of date, so unrecognizable. Miss Alcott is con-

tent to be typical. All her people have the same
background, live in the same atmosphere, profess the same ideals. Moreover, they were
ideals and an atmosphere that imposed themselves widely during their period. Mr. Howells
gives us modern instances in plenty, but no-
where does he give us clearly the quintessential
New England village. It is precisely the familiar experiences of life in that quintessential
village that Miss Alcott gives us, with careless
accuracy, without *arrière-pensée*. And it must
be remembered that, in spite of Dr. Holmes's
brave and appropriating definitions of aristocracy, and the urbanity which the descendants of
our great New Englanders would fain per-
suade us their ancestors possessed, our great
New Englanders were essentially villagers, and
that the very best thing to be said of them is
that they wrought out village life to an almost
Platonic perfection of type. "Town" will not
do to express the Boston, the Cambridge, the
Salem, the Concord, of an earlier time: it
smacks too much of London—and freedom.
The Puritans founded villages; and, spiritually
speaking, the villages that they founded are
villages still. The village that Miss Alcott knew
best was Concord; and if, for our present purpose, we find it convenient to call Concord
typical of New England, we shall certainly not
be doing New England any injustice.

As I say, what strikes one on first re-reading

her, is the extraordinary success with which
she has given us our typical New England.
Some of her books, obviously, are less successful in this way than others — *Under the
Lilacs,* for example, or *Jack and Jill,* where
(one cannot but agree with her severer critics)
there is an inexcusable amount of love-making.
There is an equally inexcusable amount of
love-making, it is interesting to remember,
in much of the earlier Howells. But for contemporary record of manners and morals, you
will go far before you match her masterpiece,
Little Women. What Meg, Jo, Beth, Amy,
and Laurie do not teach us about life in New
England at a certain time, we shall never learn
from any collected edition of the letters of
Emerson, Thoreau, or Hawthorne.

The next—and equally astounding—result
of re-reading Miss Alcott was, for me, the unexpected and not wholly pleasant corrobora-
tion of what my friend had said about her
characters. They were, in some ways, underbred. Bronson Alcott (or shall we say Mr.
March?) quotes Plato in his family circle; but
his family uses inveterately bad grammar.
"Don't talk about 'labelling' Pa, as if he was a
pickle-bottle!"—thus Jo chides her little sister
for a malapropism. Bad grammar we might
expect from Jo, as a wilful freak; but should
we expect the exquisite Amy (any little girl
will tell you how exquisite Amy is supposed to

be) to write to her father from Europe, about buying gloves in Paris, "Don't that sound sort of elegant and rich?"

The bad grammar, in all the books, is constant. And yet, I know of no other young people's stories, anywhere, wherein the background is so unbrokenly and sincerely "literary." Cheap literature is unsparingly satirized; Plato and Goethe are quoted quite as everyday matters; and "a metaphysical streak had unconsciously got into" Jo's first novel. In *The Rose in Bloom,* Miss Alcott misquotes Swinburne, to be sure, but she does it in the interest of morality; and elsewhere Mac quotes other lines from the same poet correctly. Of course, we all remember that Emerson's *Essays* helped on, largely, Mac's wooing— if, indeed, they did not do the whole trick. And has there ever been an "abode of learning"—to slip, for a moment, into the very style of *Jo's Boys*—like unto Plumfield, crowned by "Parnassus"? After all, too, we must remember how familiarly even those madcaps, Ted and Josie, bandied about the names of Greek gods. The boys and girls who scoff at the simple amusements of Miss Alcott's young heroes and heroines are, alack! not so much at home with classical mythology as the young people they despise. Yet, as I say, the bad grammar is everywhere — even in the mouths of the educators.

Breeding is, of course, not merely a matter of speech; and I fancy that my friend referred even more specifically to their manners—their morals being unimpeachable. Miss Alcott's people are, as the author herself says of them, unworldly. They are even magnificently so; and they score the worldly at every turn. You remember Mrs. March's strictures on the Moffats? and Polly's justifiable criticisms of Fanny Shaw's friends? and Rose's utter lack of snobbishness about Phœbe, the little scullery-maid, who eventually was brought up with her? Of course, Archie's mother objects, at first, to his marrying Phœbe, but she is soon reconciled—and apologetic.

Granted their unworldliness, their high scale of moral values, where, then, is the trace of vulgarity that is needed to make breeding bad? They pride themselves on their separation from all vulgarity. "My mother is a lady," Polly reflects, "even if"—even if she is not rich, like the Shaws. The March girls are always consoling themselves for their vicissitudes by the fact that their parents are gentlefolk. Well, they are underbred in precisely the way in which, one fancies, the contemporaries of Emerson in Concord may well have been underbred. It is the "plain-living" side of the "high thinking." They despised externals, and, in the end, externals had their revenge. Breeding, as such, is simply not a product of the

independent village. (Some one may mention
Cranford; but you cannot call Cranford independent, with its slavish adherence to the etiquette of the Honourable Mrs. Jamieson, its
constant awed reference to Sir Peter Arley
and the "county families.") The villagers have
not—and who supposes that Bronson Alcott
and Thoreau had it?—the gift of civilized
contacts. A contact, be it remembered, is not
quite the same thing as a relation. Manners
are a natural growth of courts. Recall any
mediæval dwelling of royalty; then imagine
life lived in those cramped chambers, in the
perpetual presence of superiors and inferiors
alike—and lived informally!

In Miss Alcott's world, all that is changed.
According to the older tradition, a totally unchaperoned youth would mean lack of breeding. Here, on the contrary, all the heroines are
unchaperoned, while the match-making mamma
is anathema. We did not cut off King Charles's
head for nothing. The reward of the unchaperoned daughter is to make a good match. In
that rigid school, conventions are judged—and
nobly enough, Heaven knows! — from the
point of view of morals alone (of absolute,
not of historic or evolutionary morals) and
many conventions are thereby damned. The
result is a little like what one has heard of
contemporary Norway. "Underbred" is very
likely too strong a word; yet one does see how

[189]

the social state described in *Little Women*
might easily shock any one brought up in a less
provincial tradition. There is too much love-
making, for example. Though sweethearting
between five-year-olds is frowned on, sweethearting between fifteen-year-olds is quite the
thing. In real life, it would not always be safe
to marry, very young, your first playmate. Any
one who has lived in the more modern New
England village knows perfectly well that
people still marry, very young, their first playmates, and that disaster often results. Nor can
Una always depend on the protection of a lion
that is necessarily invisible. Granted that Jo's
precocious sense was right, and that it would
have been a mistake for her to marry Laurie;
which of us believes that, in real life, she would
not have made the mistake? You cannot depend on young things in their teens to foresee
the future of their temperaments accurately.
One cannot but feel that if Mrs. March really
saw the complete unfitness of those two for
each other, it was her duty to put a few conventional obstacles in their path.

Perhaps all this was part of what my friend
meant by lack of breeding in the traditional
sense: the social *laissez-aller* in extraordinary
(and perhaps not eternally maintainable?)
combination with moral purity. But I suspect
that she referred, as well, to another aspect
of Miss Alcott's environment: to the unmistak-

able lack of the greater and lesser amenities of life. The plain living is quite as prominent as the high thinking. The whole tissue of the March girls' lives is a very commonplace fabric. You know that their furniture was bad— and that they did not know it; that their æsthetic sense was untrained and crude—and that they did not care; that the simplicity of their meals, their household' service, their dress, their every day manners (in spite of the myth about Amy) was simplicity of the common, not of the intelligent, kind. You really would not want to spend a week in the house of any one of them. Nor had their simplicity in any wise the quality of austerity. Remember the pies that the older March girls carried for muffs (the management whereof was one of the ever unsolved riddles of my childhood).

No: in so far as breeding is a matter of externals, one must admit that there is some sense in calling Miss Alcott's people underbred. Perhaps we do not choose to call breeding a matter of externals. In that, we should perfectly agree with Miss Alcott's people themselves; and to that we shall presently come. For what is incontrovertible is that Miss Alcott's work is a genuine document.

I have spoken of the unimpeachable morality of Miss Alcott's world. Charlie lost Rose for having drunk one glass of champagne too much. That is the worst sin committed in any of the books, so far as I remember. Of course, the black sheep, Dan, had been in prison; but he had killed his man inevitably, almost helplessly, in self-defence; and besides, the treatment of Dan is purely snobbish, from start to finish. Even Mrs. Jo, while she stands by him, is acutely conscious of the social difference between him and her own kin. The moment he lifts his eyes to Bess—! No: the books are quite snobbish enough, in their way. Nat, foundling and fiddler, is permitted to marry Daisy in the end (though, really, anybody might have married Daisy!). But Nat, though a *parvenu,* is a milksop, and is quite able to say that he has never done anything really disgraceful. The fact is that their social distinctions, while they operate socially, are yet all moral in origin. And this is a very "special" note: the bequest, it may well be, of Calvin.

> We're the elect, and you'll be damned;
> Hell, like a wallet, shall be crammed
> With God's own reprobates.

The transcendental Mr. March would never have sung it; but he and his knew something akin to those resolute discriminations.

Another point is perhaps even more interesting. There are not, I believe, any other books in the world so blatantly full of morality—of moral issues, and moral tests, and morals passionately abided by—and at the same time so empty of religion. The Bible is never quoted; almost no one goes to church; and they pray only when very young and in extreme cases. The only religious allusion, so far as I know, in *Little Women,* is the patronizing mention of the Madonna provided for Amy by Aunt March's Catholic maid. And even then, you can see how broad-minded Mrs. March considers herself, to permit Amy the quasi-oratory; and Amy does not attempt to disguise the fact that she admires the picture chiefly for its artistic quality. Yet it is only fair to remember that, in Miss Alcott's day, people were reading, without so much as one grain of salt, the confessions of "escaped" nuns, and the novels of Mrs. Julia McNair Wright—and that Elsie Dinsmore developed brain fever when her father threatened to send her to a convent school. Perhaps Mrs. March had a right to flatter herself. Again, as I say, these are documents.

There are many other straws to show which way the wind blows. Would any one but Miss Alcott, for example, have allowed her chief heroine to marry a Professor Bhaer? No modern child ever quite recovers from the shock of it. But we must remember that, in Miss Alcott's time, German metaphysicians were not without honor in Concord. The breath of reform, too, is hot upon the pages. "Temperance"—remember Charlie's unlucky glass of champagne, and Laurie's promise to Meg on her wedding-day; the festivals of the virtuous are a perpetual bath of lemonade. "Woman Suffrage"—recall the discussions alluded to in "The Pickwick Portfolio," and the fate of the few scoffers in co-educational Plumfield. The children are all passionate little Abolitionists; and the youths are patriotic with a fervid, unfamiliar patriotism, which touches, at its dim source, emotions that to us are almost more prehistoric than historic.

In the minds of Miss Alcott's world, there is still a lively distrust of the British. They are wont to oppress their colonies, and they cheat at croquet. Indeed, Miss Alcott's characters look a little askance at all foreigners—except German professors. There is no prophecy of the Celtic Revival in their condescending charity to poor Irishwomen. The only people, not themselves, whom they wholly respect, are the negroes. The rich men are nearly all East India merchants, and their money goes eventually to endow educational institutions. The young heroes have a precocious antipathy to acquiring wealth for its own sake. Demi would rather, he says, sweep door-mats in a publishing-house than go into business, like "Stuffy" and his kind. "I would rather be a door-keeper in the house of the Lord"—it would hardly over-emphasize Demi's so typical feeling for the sanctity of the printed page; for the utter desirability of the publisher's own office, where, as he says, great men go in and out, with respect. And—to complete the evidence—the books do not lack the note of New English austerity, though they come by it indirectly enough. The New English literary tradition seems to be fairly clear: either passion must be public, or, if it is private, it must be thwarted. There is a good deal of public passion — for philanthropy, for education, and what-not—in the books, after all. There is no private passion at all: though the books brim with sentiment, Miss Alcott writes as one who had never loved. It would be difficult to find, anywhere, stories so full of love-making and so empty of emotion.

Straws show which way the wind blows; and these straws are all borne in the same direction. Is not this the New England on which, if not in which, we were all brought up? Any honest New Englander — a New Englander of the villages, I mean—will admit that the New English are singularly ungifted for social life and manners. We suspected that long ago, when we first read Miss Alcott, if we happened to turn, after *Little Women,* to any one of Mrs. Ewing's or Mrs. Molesworth's stories. Imagine Jo dressed, as Mrs. Molesworth's heroines all were, by Walter Crane! The real "old-fashioned girl" was not Polly Milton, but Griselda, in *The Cuckoo*

Clock. Polly was simply of no fashion at all. There was some (wistful?) sense of this in us, even then. Yet of course we admitted that, in comparison, Mrs. Molesworth lacked plot— as Heaven knows she did! Any New Englander of the villages is familiar, too, with the passion for "education"; a passion that, I suspect, you can match now only in the Middle West. We all know that bigoted scholarliness, in combination, precisely, with nasal and ungrammatical speech, which there is no special point in flattering with the term "idiomatic." One or two of Mr. Churchill's novels have preserved to us instances of it. We are fortunate if we have come off quite free of the superstition, so prevalent through the March family, that a book — "any old" book — is sacred. We scoff heartily at the *parvenu* whose books are bound without first being printed; but I am not sure that any pure-bred villager would not rather have sham books than no books at all. We cannot help it. No other furniture seems to us quite so good.

We have all been brought up, too, to be moral snobs. New England mothers must often be put to it to find purely moral grounds for discriminating against some of the playmates their children would ignorantly bring home. They must often yearn to say, without indirection, "I do not wish you to play with the butcher's little girl, and her being in your Sunday-school class makes no difference whatever." But the real New England mother never does. She must manage it otherwise; since the only legitimate basis for her discriminations would be some sort of proof that butchers' little girls were apt to be naughty. The respective fates of Nat and Dan are, I dare to say, as accurate as if they had been recorded by the official investigators of the Eugenics Society. The lack of religion, some one may object, is anything but typically New English. Perhaps, a hundred years ago, it would not have been. And we have not, to be sure, been transcendental with impunity: we have the Calvinistic Unitarian. But the average New England conscience has always had a more natural turn for ethics than for pure piety. Children in Miss Alcott's books were brought up like ourselves, to obey their parents. It was Elsie Dinsmore, on her Southern plantation, who (like a Presbyterian St. Rose of Lima) defied her father for religion's sake. Of course we all had to read about Elsie surreptitiously. We knew that without asking. There was a good deal of plain thinking, as well as of high thinking, in our and Miss Alcott's world. As for our unworldliness: we have come a long way since Miss Alcott; yet I verily believe that, even now, almost any bounder can take us in if he poses as a philosopher. So many have done it!

I have not done more than indicate Miss

Alcott's exceeding fidelity. Begin recalling her for yourself, and you will agree that she gives us social life as New Englanders, for decades, have, on the whole, known it. The relations of parent and child, brother and sister, community and individual, of playmates, of lovers, of citizens, are all such as we know them. They are familiar to us, if not positively in our own experience. Life has grown more complicated everywhere. Yet I doubt if, even now, any New English child would instinctively call Miss Alcott's people underbred. We still understand their code, if we do not practise it. New England is still something more than a convenient term for map-makers. These be our own villages.

THE SENSUAL EAR

I HAVE a friend who always calls—when he remembers to, for alas! he sometimes forgets—the Methodist Church building in our village, a "conventicle." I wish he did not sometimes forget, for nothing makes me so at peace with my hereditary nonconformity as to hear an Anglican imply, by such verbal affectations, what he thinks of the dissidence of dissent. Methodism is as foreign to me as Anglicanism; yet, I doubt not, the Epworth League sings, in its handsome "conventicle," just the hymns that of old were sung by the Y. P. S. C. E. It is many a year since I attended a Y. P. S. C. E. meeting; and I have an idea—it is almost a fear—that *Gospel Hymns, No.* 5, is by this time *Gospel Hymns, No.* 10, and that some of the most haunting melodies are gone therefrom. Perhaps the "Endeavorers" are now chanting *Hymns Ancient and Modern.* But I hope not. Oh, I cannot think it!

When life grows very dreary; when the Hindenburg line seems to turn from shadow to substance; when the Council of Workmen's and Soldiers' Deputies has indulged in a new "democratic" vagary; when flour has gone up two dollars more a barrel and the priceless potato is but a soggy pearl, deserving to be cast before swine; when another member of

the family has broken a leg or had appendi-
citis—then my husband (he, too, of yore an
"Endeavorer") and I are wont to burst, simultaneously, mechanically, unthinking and uncon-
spiring, into song. And the songs we hear each
other humming in separate recesses of the
house are *Gospel Hymns.* Humming, we
converge upon the drawing-room from our different retreats; and sometimes we look each
other in the eye and say hardily, "Let's." Then
we sit down and incite each other to a desperate vocalism. We see how many we can remember, out of our evangelistic youth, and we sing
them all. We remember a good many, if truth
be told; and once I found a rapt huddle of colored servants on the stair-landing getting a
free "revival." Neither of us has a voice worth
mentioning, so I think that we must, without
realizing it, have reproduced the fervor along
with the words.

They were cannily arranged, those Moody
and Sankey hymns: if you sing them at all, you
cannot help pounding down on the essential
words. They wallow in beat and accent. "A
Shelter in the *Time* of *Storm.*" We usually
begin with that. It is ineluctable. But oh, how
I wish that either of us could remember more
than one "verse" of

> Well, wife, I've found the model church,
>   And worshipped there to-day;
> It made me think of good old times
>   Before my hair was gray.

I have never heard it sung—I never "belonged" to the Y. P. S. C. E.—but my husband says that he has. My husband also says that he has heard "the trundle-bed one." I do not believe it, though he is a truthful man. I cannot believe it; the less, that he remembers none of the words, and that it is only I, who recall, visually, in the lower corner of a page,—

Poking (perhaps it was another verb) 'mid the dust and
    rafters
There I found my trundle-bed.

A slight altercation always develops here. Why should he be more royalist than the king? It is not conceivable that it was ever *sung*; and even he cannot remember the tune; so we join forces in "To the Work, to the Work," or "There Shall Be Showers of Blessing."

(Mercy-drops round us are *fall*-ing,
    But for the *showers* we plead.)

He has an uncanny and inexplicable prejudice against "God Be with You Till We Meet Again"—perhaps because they always sang it for the last one. But I can usually get him to "oblige" with a solo—"Throw Out the Life-Line"—which I am sure was not in "No. 5," because we never, never sang it; though I do remember hearing a returning delegate to a Y. P. S. C. E. convention say that it was the one "the people of Montreal seemed to like best." Somewhere in the nineties, Endeavorers in

thousands sang it all up and down Sherbrooke
Street, apparently. Well: I am like the people
of Montreal. It always "gets" me, in the dissenting marrow of my dissenting soul; and
when my husband has "obliged" me with it, I
am ready to forget the Council of Workmen's
and Soldiers' Deputies. What *can* the devil do
in the face of "Throw Out the Life-Line," and
its "linked sweetness long drawn out"?

By all of which it is made evident that, in
the matter of hymns, mine is the "sensual ear."
(Not so my husband's: he sings them in the
critical spirit, as he might illustrate a violation
of rhetoric. He loathes "Throw Out the Life-
Line," even while the chorus makes his voice
appeal and yearn in spite of him. As I said, he
does it only to oblige.) The church of my
choosing, if not of my profession, is the same
as that of my friend who talks of "conventicles." There I sing *Hymns Ancient and
Modern* (or that American corruption thereof,
the *Hymnal*) with the most conforming.
And certainly, except for a few time-honored
chants which they share with all Dissenters,
their hymns are to me "ditties of no tone."
My husband disagrees with me; but he is
not, equally with me, the predestined prey of
the brass band. He is better educated than I;
has listened oftener at twilight to the enchanted choirs of New College and Magdalen.
He likes the non-committal melodies of the

Hymnal far, far better than the sentimental *parti pris* of *Gospel Hymns*.

I know as well as he does that the sentimental quality is of a sort that ought not to be there at all. I know that the music of "Throw Out the Life-Line" belongs morally with the music of "Old Black Joe," and "Oh, Promise Me," and "There'll Be a Hot Time in the Old Town To-night." I know that the appeal of that tune is sensuous and emotional and personal, and, for a hymn, all, all wrong. I realize that, for' church, Gregorian is the only wear; and that the less you diverge therefrom, the more decent you are. I, too, prefer Bach and Palestrina, and, for congregational singing, the oldest Latin hymns you can get. I can even see that the aridity and sameness of the Anglican "hymn-tunes" are more dignified, and more to the purpose, than the plangent and catchy refrains by which Sankey lured "wandering boys" back to be safe-folded with "the ninety and nine." And yet, when my husband (by request) croons "Throw Out the Life-Line," I cannot resist. I am evangelized.

True, I perceived this perniciousness early. Perhaps the white light dawned on me when, in Y. P. S. C. E. days, an older friend (who was in love) confided to me that the words of a certain Gospel Hymn seemed to her not altogether reverent: they could so easily be applied to a human love-affair. She was quite right, I think. Some of us have felt the same about Crashaw and Giles Fletcher. But though the words were, in all conscience, carnal enough, I believe it was the tune that did the trick and set her dreaming of her young hero.

> For I am his, and he is mine,
> Forever and forever.

Oh, the yearning of that refrain: slow and honeyed and melancholy as "My Old Kentucky Home" or "Way Down Upon the Suwanee River"! Musically, doubtless, not so good; but musically of the same school, and suggestive— it, too—of plantations and moonlight and banjos and rich, heart-rending negro voices. My friend was right: they are not in the best tradition of reverence, those Moody and Sankey hymns. And yet—here's the rub—why do we remember them, when all but the most universal of the hymns we sang in church and sang much oftener than these, have gone beyond recapturing? My husband resents remembering them; he would far rather remember more worthy things. But I do not: I would not, for anything, lose them out of the rag-bag which is my mind. I am not sure I would not rather lose certain stanzas from the Greek Anthology, which come to my lips in much the same unvolitional fashion. From those refrains I reconstruct a whole moral and social world, even as

Cuvier reconstructed his mastodon. You remember what the "Evening Hymn" did for Mottram and Lowndes in "The End of the Passage"? Just that "I Know that My Redeemer Lives" does for me. And—this is the point—"Rock of Ages" and "Holy, Holy, Holy," do not do it; though I knew these even earlier, and am still, on occasion, singing them. So it is not all a question of association and the power of youthful memories. It is the very quality of the music—the words were negligible, when they were not atrocious—that touched in me, and can still touch, something popular, emotional, vulgar; something very low-brow and democratic, not to say mobbish. "The sensual ear."

Even in youth, I had the sense to differentiate. "Jerusalem the Golden," discovered in another hymn-book than our own, was for many years my favorite hymn—even during those years when I was singing "Beulah Land" and " Wonderful Words of Life." I knew it was better; I knew I liked it better; I knew that it had more to do with religion than all the "Beulah Lands" ever written. True, the words helped; and the words of the Gospel Hymns were a hindrance, even then. But my soul recognized the validity, the reality of the music. "Jerusalem the Golden" remained my favorite until "The Son of God Goes Forth to War" succeeded it in my affections; always to be, until I die, my very favorite. And even while we sang—

> And view the shining glory shore,
> My heaven, my home, for evermore.

I had memories of something still better than "Jerusalem the Golden": memories of an interval in a French convent where we chanted the Magnificat to its proper plain-song. Though, even there—but I shall come to that later.

Not long ago, we had a friend staying with us who was bred a Romanist. How Moody and Sankey got mentioned, I do not know—but they did; and our friend insisted that Moody and Sankey could not conceivably be so bad as the modern Catholic hymns. We exclaimed; she reaffirmed. There was nothing for it but to put the burning question to the proof. Quietly, by the fire, we staged a little contest. We sang our Gospel Hymns; and she—well, she sang dreadful things. There was in particular a hymn to St. Joseph, beloved of sodalities. . . . No, I think her "exhibit" was really worse than ours. It had the rag-time flatness without the rag-time catchiness, or the crooning negro quality. Bred up in part on such modern by-products of the Holy Catholic Church, no wonder that she succumbed utterly to my husband's rendition of "Throw Out the Life-Line." "I think it's lovely," she said; siding with me, to his great chagrin. How I wished that our friend of the "conventicles" were there to decide between us—he who in his youth was forbidden to accompany his friends to Y. P. S. C. E. meetings as he might have been forbidden to go to dime-museums. But he has no ear—"sensual"or other. Perhaps he could not have helped.

Our Catholic friend's exhibit gave me pause. I knew that in France they sing, nowadays, hymns unworthy of Gothic architecture. Not so many years ago, in a beautiful French cathedral which I was by way of frequenting, I heard the children of some sodality or confraternity pouring forth as poor a piece of holy rag-time as any conventicle has ever echoed. It jerked me back into the past, violently, as Hassan's carpet must have jerked its fortunate owner through space.

> Vierge, notre espérance,
>   Étends sur nous ton bras,
> Sauve, sauve la France,
>   Ne l'abandonne pas,
>   Ne l'abandonne pas.

So we sang it, too, at the Assomption, in happier days, each with a veil and a candle, winding in and out among the green alleys of the convent park. But the young Tourangeaux went on to sing worse things: songs less catholic, more evangelical, with words more bitter and tones more shrill. I escaped, to return only

at the hour of Benediction, when I knew that
the "O Salutaris Hostia" and "Tantum Ergo"
would mount again with the incense towards
the rich mediæval windows.

I fear it is true, as our Catholic friend said,
that the Church has fallen musically, as it has
done architecturally, on evil days. Well: these
shrill and senseless tunes are their equivalent
for our Moody and Sankey. Even in conventicles, we have more dignified hymn-books for
use in "church" as opposed to Sunday-school or
Y. P. S. C. E., and the like. And as our Pri-
mary Department (of the Sunday-school) was
handed over to the works of Fanny Crosby
(did she write

> Roses in bloom,
> Filling the room,
> With perfume rich and rare.

I wonder? Anyhow, she wrote most of them),
so the young Catholics in both France and
America are handed over to the musical diva-
gations of ill-educated priests. It is a pity; for
they have a tradition that cannot be bettered.
My ancestors sang lustily out of the old *Bay
Psalm Book :*

> Ye monsters of the mighty deep,
> Your Maker's praises spout;
> Up from the sands ye codlings peep,
> And wag your tails about.

But, at the same period, *their* ancestors were
singing the Latin hymns of the Middle Ages in

undegenerate solemnity. It is natural enough, perhaps, that I should have emerged on "There's a Light in the Valley for Me"; but why should they have emerged on "Souvenez-vous, Jésus," and the Mariolatrous wailing of "Im-mac-u-late, Im-mac-u-late"? Take as fine a Protestant hymn as, on the whole, we have inherited—"O God, Our Help in Ages Past." Its tune is, to my thinking, bad: difficult to sing and monotonous to hear. But in the very church that these poor French infants are innocently desecrating, a few hours, more or less, see a whole congregation chanting, with passionless and awful reverence,

Parce, Domine, parce populo tuo; nec in æternum irascaris nobis.

Whoever has heard that welling slowly from crowded choir, nave, and transept, the coifed peasant and the trained *séminariste* singing in unison (no staginess of part-singing there!), and has joined his voice to the multitudinous supplication, will not cease to regret that modern vulgarity is as Catholic as it is Protestant.

It was the most delightful of Huysmans's perversities to contend, in all seriousness, that the Devil, driven out of an immemorial haunt of his own near Lourdes by the advent in that spot of the Blessed Virgin, took his sullen revenge on the æsthetic sense of her priests. He could no longer hold his filthy Sabbaths there; but he could and did bewitch the clergy into making Lourdes a thing of ugliness. Their taste went wrong with everything they touched in Lourdes; and while Satan could not prevent the Blessed Virgin from working miracles, he could still bring it about that the faithful should be healed amid the most hideous architectural surroundings. Perhaps Huysmans would have credited the modern Catholic music unhesitatingly to the devil.

But certainly Moody and Sankey were not clerics of Lourdes. Nor could the Presbyterians who first sang the rhymed version of the Twenty-Third Psalm to the air of "So bin ich vergessen, vergessen bin ich" be suspected of any part in the Devil's private feuds with the Virgin. Indeed, the particular Presbyterians whom I have heard sing it thus had not, I fancy, much more reverence for the one than for the other.

I do not think that we can account for *Gospel Hymns No. 5* by the Huysmans formula. Even the hymn to St. Joseph, beloved of sodalities, is, I believe, mere modern pandering to the uncultured majority: revivalism in essence, like Moody and Sankey and the Salvation Army and Billy Sunday. But at least the Catholics have this advantage: that though they too have indulged in operatic music and have even sunk to "Vierge, notre espérance," they still hear from their choirs the ancient music and the ancient words. You lose the sodalities and confraternities when you hear once more the familiar "Tantum Ergo" (I do not mean the florid one that they sing at St. Roch in Paris, and elsewhere); the new vulgarity is forgotten, as many vulgarities have been touched and then forgotten by Rome, in her time.

I used to think that the worst of our bad Protestant hymns was their ignoring of the human intelligence.

> Many giants great and tall,
> Stalking through the land,
> Headlong to the earth would fall
> If met by Daniel's Band.

(My fortunate husband sang it in his youth.) But even that, while it could have a religious meaning, I should say, only for a sub-normal intelligence, is not a deliberate and explicit defiance of the intellect of man.

> Verbum caro, panem verum
> Verbo carnem efficit:
> Fitque sanguis Christi merum;
> Et si sensus deficit,
> Ad firmandum cor sincerum
> Sola fides sufficit.

> Tantum ergo sacramentum
> Veneremur cernui,
> Et antiquum documentum
> Novo cedat ritui:
> Præstet fides supplementum
> Sensuum defectui.

It took St. Thomas Aquinas, Doctor Angelicus, thus to state, in one supreme utterance, the whole case against the Higher Criticism.

No, I do not think that the sense of a hymn counts so much. The mediæval "Ave Maris Stella" has not much more to recommend it, philosophically speaking, than the hymn with the "Im-mac-u-late, Im-mac-u-late" refrain. A poem, even a religious poem, is good poetry or bad poetry, and that is all there is to it. "From Greenland's Icy Mountains" is a silly poem, and "The Son of God Goes Forth to War" is a rather fine poem; and Bishop Heber wrote both. But the permanent superiority of the latter is in the music to which it is set. One Presbyterian sect sings, I believe, nothing but the Psalms—rather unfortunately metricized, to be sure—and their church singing is the dreariest in the world. Yet the Psalms are rated high. "Onward, Christian Soldiers" gets its appeal from Sir Arthur Sullivan and not from the author. I do not believe that "Nearer, My God, to Thee" would have been the favorite hymn of the late President McKinley were it not for the slow, swinging tempo, which needs only a little quickening to be an excellent waltz, with all the emotional appeal of good waltz music.

On the whole, *Hymns Ancient and Modern* are far better, from the point of view of poetry, than *Gospel Hymns, No. 5* — but they have not converted half so many people. The elect, the high-brows, may say what they like: if you are doing your evangelizing on the grand scale, the "sensual ear" must be pleased. I do not believe that the music I have referred to, of the "Tantum Ergo" or the "Parce, Domine," would ever convert the crowd in a tent or a tabernacle—even if D. L. Moody or Fanny Crosby wrote new words to it. But if you let a grammar-school pupil hack words out of the New Testament and set them to the tune of "Massa's in the Cold, Cold Ground"—well, it would be strange if some one were not converted. You may be very sure that the Roman Catholic Church has not taken to vulgar and catchy hymns without a set purpose of winning souls.

> At the Cross, at the Cross, where I first saw the light
> And the burden of my sin rolled away,
> It was there by faith I received my sight,
> And now I am happy all the day.

The last line might almost have been lifted bodily from one of Stephen Foster's negro melodies. It has the very lilt of

> My old Kentucky home far away.

And it is only one of many in *Gospel Hymns, No. 5*. That is why my husband remembers them, in spite of himself. He may contemn them, but he cannot forgot. There is hardly

[213]

one of them that would not consort happily with the right kind of brass band. They connote crowds and the "emotion of multitude." So, to me, does the "Parce, Domine" connote crowds—but crowds awe-struck, unweeping, and in no mood for stimulation by a cornet accompaniment. There is a cardinal difference. The success of almost any Gospel Hymn depends on an emotional appeal very like that of Kipling's banjo:

> And the tunes that mean so much to you alone—
> Common tunes that make you choke and blow your nose,
> Vulgar tunes that bring the laugh that brings the groan—
> I can rip your very heartstrings out with those.

Whatever Bach and Palestrina and Scarlatti and good Gregorian do to you—well, it is not that. Whereas almost any good Gospel Hymn gets you, if it gets you at all, in the banjo way. There is the revivalistic essence in all of them. And when the Catholics wish to be revivalistic, they imitate, rather badly, the Protestant "hymn-tune."

Most of my friends are so truly high-brow that they cannot be "got" in the banjo way. They do not like cornet solos; and brass bands playing negro-melodies leave them dry-eyed. They honestly prefer the Kniesel Quartet or a Brahms symphony. Their arid and exquisite æstheticism rejects these low appeals. Did I not say that my husband loathes "Throw Out the Life-Line" even while he is reducing me to an emotional crumple? I refuse to admit that I am incapable of that same arid and exquisite æstheticism; but the lower appeal reaches me too. I do weep over the brass bands. I do choke over the flag appropriately carried. I do fall in love (if I am careful to shut my eyes) with a good tenor voice. And while there are, luckily, a great many people like my husband, there must be millions more like me. He remembers the Gospel Hymns; but I like them.

Not quite to the trail-hitting point; but then I fancy the hymns of the tabernacle are less good than they used to be. I do not know the tune of "Brighten the Corner Where You Are." Though my six-year-old son has learned it from the cook, I do not believe he has the tune right. He cannot have it right: if it were right, there would be no sawdust trail. Nor do I know the music of "The Brewer's Big Horses Cannot Roll Over Me." But I have a suspicion that Billy Sunday's hymns are nothing like so good as Moody and Sankey. The dance music of the day always has its effect on popular airs of every kind, even religious. I venture to say (*pace* the shade of Lord Byron) that the waltz, throughout the nineteenth century, had a strong religious influence. Every one knows that good waltz music, if played slowly enough, is the saddest thing in the world. The emotion aroused by good waltz music well played is blood-brother to the emotion aroused by "God Be with You Till We Meet Again" and "For You I Am Praying, I'm Praying for You." Waltzes and Gospel Hymns reinforce each other—which is probably why the unco' guid object to dancing. But with all due allowances for mob-emotion and the sensual ear, I cannot believe that syncopation serves the Lord. People's eyes do not grow dim as they listen to a fox-trot. It does nothing to bring forth that melting sense of universal love which the old popular music did. All waltz music was in essence melancholy; and all sentimental melancholies meet together somewhere in the recesses of the vulgar heart. Yes: when popular composers were writing good waltzes, it was easier for the Sankeys and Blisses to write good hymns. The Y. P. S. C. E. must have had easier work with the young people who were singing "Marguerite," than it has now with the young people who are singing "At the Garbage Gentlemen's Ball." I have a notion that the young people who are singing "At the Garbage Gentlemen's Ball" do not go to Y. P. S. C. E. meetings at all. Well, you see, those who sang "Marguerite" did.

Those who know say that we are growing more vulgar all the time. Perhaps the difference between D. L. Moody and Billy Sunday is a good index of that degeneration. Certainly the silly young things who wept while they sang "God Be with You Till We Meet Again" would not have pretended to call Christ up on the telephone—or have permitted any one else to do it in their presence. But, thank Heaven, the conventicles are like to outlast the tabernacle.

At all events, I am sure of one thing: that my husband will not be persuaded, twenty years hence, to "oblige" with "The Brewer's Big Horses." But I hope he will continue at intervals to oblige with "Throw Out the Life-Line." For, so long as he does, I shall continue to be evangelized.

BRITISH NOVELISTS, LTD.

I WAS reading a novel, the other day; had got about half way through it. The novel in question was by one of the younger English authors. It was very odd, I thought to myself as I perused it, that I should not (for I read a great deal of fiction) have read before anything by Mr. D. H. Lawrence. I had always meant to, but his work had, for some reason or other, not come my way. And I was glad I was reading it. I ought to have done D. H. Lawrence before. Some people had told me he was "different." He was not so different as all that; still, there was something fresh about him. Perhaps one could differentiate within that group, though I had long since despaired of doing so. I would certainly get something else of D. H. Lawrence's. At that point I decided to go to bed, and shut the book up smartly. The cover revealed to me that the author was J. D. Beresford. Why I had ever thought it was D. H. Lawrence, I do not know. Some false association of ideas at the moment of borrowing it, probably.

The joke is on me, as the younger generation would say. And yet, there is something to be said on my side. The fact is that I had not expected D. H. Lawrence to be one whit different from Hugh Walpole, J. D. Beresford, Compton Mackenzie, Gilbert Cannan, Oliver Onions, and W. L. George. I found, I thought, a little difference: not much, but enough to give one hope. To be sure, the hope would have ebbed, in any case, before the book was finished. My only gain was the knowledge that Mr. Beresford can do something besides Jacob Stahl. I have yet to experience D. H. Lawrence. Still, I submit that when, to distinguish between one author and another, you are satisfied with so tiny a difference in style as appears between two works by the same man, it means that differences in style within that particular group are not very startling. One would never have read half of *Tess* and taken it for the work of Henry James; or half of *Nostromo* and taken that for the work of Meredith. One would have been brought up standing at the first page. It may be, as I say, that D. H. Lawrence is going to be to me, some day, a revelation of individuality. But the reviews do not give one much hope of that.

Now, there are three authors in England who stand a little away from this larger group, though they are not precisely contemporaries of Hardy or of Conrad. Wells and Bennett and Galsworthy have some individuality of style. A chapter of Mr. Wells is "different." A chapter of Arnold Bennett or of Mr. Galsworthy is different. Or let me put it in this way. You would not get through half of any one of Mr. Wells's later novels without a deal of pseudo-philosophical reflection on the scheme of things. You would not read so far in any book by Mr. Arnold Bennett without meeting and recognizing his peculiar kind of humor: semi-grin, semi-farcical. And I am sure that you would not get through many chapters of a typical Galsworthy novel without hearing a bird calling to its mate —not if there were a human love affair going on. I do not think you could comfortably sit down with any one of them for half an evening and think that you were reading D. H. Lawrence. You would know whom you were reading.

These three gentlemen have, of course, been writing longer than the aforesaid younger group. They are, one might say, the elder brothers of the brood. If any one of them has served as model to the younger fry, it is Mr. Wells. None of the younger fry has ever approached the technical excellence of *Kipps*; but, on the other hand, almost any one of them could have written *Ann Veronica*. Mr. Wells has certainly led them all astray in his time. But there is another equally important thing to be said: Mr. Wells has gone on. In his later phases, he stands quite apart from them all. *The Research Magnificent* and *Mr. Britling Sees It Through* are perfectly individual: they are not, and never could have been, the product of a syndicate. Time was when Wells and Bennett seemed to be drawing near each other. *Tono-Bungay* is Bennett-ish in spots; and *Bealby* is, superficially, almost straight Bennett. But Mr. Wells, for weal or woe, has always been interested in the social scheme. The most important thing in *Tono-Bungay* is Bladesover and Bladesover's moral effect; and even in the ridiculous *Bealby* there is more than an echo of Bladesover. Mr. Wells is interested in moral values. Sometimes he has had very queer notions about them; but his reward for having been perpetually preoccupied with them is to have won through to *The Research Magnificent* and *Mr. Britling.* You may not agree with the hero of either book; but at least he is a person for whom you have respect. His is a dignified moral reaction, even if it is not the moral reaction you would have preferred. He is a serious person, envisaging his relations to the world in a serious temper.

One does not see Mr. Bennett's characters thus envisaging the world; not, at all events, since *The Old Wives' Tale.* And even in *The Old Wives' Tale* you feel rather the deterministic net in which the characters are caught, than any personal decisions of their own. The moral of the book is that heredity is more powerful than environment, if these

two come to grips. In the later books, when
they are not, like *Denry the Audacious* and
Buried Alive, delicious bits of fooling, you
get men and women of a monstrous egotism,
of whom it cannot be discerned that either
heredity or environment explicitly controls
them against their will. An acute critic, who
has incidentally had his own say about Wells
and Bennett, told me the other day that he
thought Bennett's people had "character." I
should have said rather that they were "characters," in the colloquial sense. They have self-
assertiveness; like Aunty Hamps, they may sub-
jugate their world. But "character"? No: that
is a finer, more complicated possession. They
want things, sometimes good things and sometimes bad; but they are (especially the women)
blond beasts as to their methods. If there is,
on the whole, a less decent creature in modern
fiction than Hilda Lessways, or a more idiotic
one than Audrey Moze, I have still to encounter her. They invoke their gods

> By the hunger of change and emotion,
> By the thirst of unbearable things.

Ann Veronica, as I once tried to point out, is
not true to life: she is a nice girl who proceeds
to have reactions that a nice girl does not have
without a lot of intervening history. Hilda is
never a nice girl; she is a monster from the
start and to the finish. As for Audrey—*pace*

Mr. Bennett—she is a "moron," or very near it. Mr. Bennett spends more time on his female than on his male characters. He began with the evident intention of "doing" young Clayhanger. But poor Clayhanger eventually turned into Hilda's daily bread. He exists only to be masticated by her. She lifts her head from that "fiero pasto," immitigable as Ugolino.

Now, I may well be accused, by Mr. Bennett's admirers, of a belated Victorianism, because I do not like his Hildas and Leonoras and Audreys. Well, I do not like Balzac's Valérie Marneffe; yet surely *La Cousine Bette* is one of the great novels of the nineteenth century. Henry James, some years ago, drew a distinction between Thackeray and Balzac in their treatment of unpleasant characters; insisting that Thackeray did not give his a fair chance. "Balzac loved his Valérie as Thackeray did not love his Becky," said Mr. James. However much Balzac loved his Valérie, he did not love her to the point of trying to make us think her delightful. The love he bore her was a love as impersonal as the right hand of Rhadamanthus: a love that consented to be just. Balzac may have loved his Valérie as Thackeray did not love his Becky; but he did not love his Valérie as Mr. Bennett loves his Hilda and his Audrey. He loved her, that is, in a quite different sense. Mr. Bennett positively seems to think that Hilda is as decent

as any one else, and more interesting than most
people. If he does not really think so, then his
method is at fault, and his books belie him.
His method is not at fault in *Denry*, because
there is no implication anywhere that Denry
exists in a moral sense: he is a "card," and
only a "card." It is never hinted that we ought
to take him seriously. He is merely funny; the
humor of him is the moral equivalent of an
obstacle race or the pursuit of a greased pig.

If only Mr. Bennett would keep to his
Denrys! For in the realm of extravaganza he
is irresistible. Also, when he does the detail of
the Five Towns, he is delightful for sheer con-
vincingness. But he must stick to concrete detail. He must not deal with the human soul,
for when he comes to moral reactions, he shows
that he has no conception of differences. Mr.
Bennett's world, frankly, seems to me like the
world of the dead as described by the poet:

> Outside of all the worlds and ages,
> There where the fool is as the sage is,
>   There where the slayer is clean of blood;
> No end, no passage, no beginning,
> There where the sinner leaves off sinning,
>   There where the good man is not good.
>
> There is not one thing with another,
> But Evil saith to Good: My brother,
>   My brother, I am one with thee.

His world is a world where Evil saith to Good:
"My brother, I am one with thee." If he can-

not write us another *Old Wives' Tale*, we must at least hope, as I say, that he will stick to Denry and Alice Challis. *The Lion's Share* does 'not give much promise that he will do a second *Old Wives' Tale*. He has a positive fondness for mean people; people who walk blind through a world with beauty in it; people who think their own emotions supremely valuable simply because they are their own.

The realists, I know, have always contended that an author should be impersonal; that he should not have an "attitude"; that he should record life as it is, without comment. Into the possibility or impossibility of that feat (the old technical controversy) we need not go, here and now. The general opinion is that you can tell where an author stands, in spite of him. Certainly Mr. Bennett is not impersonal; he does have an attitude. Not in any of the permitted ways (comment of other characters, logical and retributive results of committed acts, etc.) does he show himself suspicious of his people's real natures, or disapproving of their odiousness. If he were only scourging, satirist-fashion, the egotism of mankind, one could bear it. But no: Mr. Bennett seems to love his Yahoos. If he does not love them, then, as I say, his methods are at fault.

Another author who has gone dwindling is Mr. Galsworthy. Tremendous hopes of him and of our permanent joy in him, we had when *The Man of Property* appeared. And, of course, one knows people who stick to him for his "style." One does not quite know why: as style, it cannot touch either Mr. Wells's or Mr. Bennett's style. I fancy it is because there will always be a perceptible number of people who are reverent before long descriptions of nature. Nature, when it gets into a book, is somehow sacred. Perhaps it is Wordsworth's fault. Literary pieties die hard. Anyhow, there always are long descriptions of nature in Mr. Galsworthy's novels, and if they are delicately confused with mating animals and human sex impulses, and all the connotation of stirring sap and swelling buds and the like, that will certainly not make them any less popular. Yet the fact is that Mr. Galsworthy has gone on, from book to book, steadily becoming more sentimental and more flabby. I am speaking here of his novels. His *Five Tales* hold their own with *The Man of Property.* His work cannot be called rich in situations, since he has never, so far, failed to repeat (I think I am not mistaken) the same situation: a man in love with some woman he has no legal right to be in love with. Often, that is a very interesting situation; but it is not the only source of drama in life, and one does get tired of it. And I do not think that Mr. Galsworthy makes it any more interesting or sympathetic by constantly involving the vegetable world, or by punctuating every declaration of unlawful love with the calls of mating birds. One is tempted to assure him that "The flowers that bloom in the spring (tra-la!) have nothing to do with the case." But the sanity of W. S. Gilbert is gone from among us.

With Thomas Hardy, one feels at least the reality of this intrusion of external nature; because, as some critic (I think, Mr. W. J. Dawson) has said, his people are children of the soil in no trite sense. They are akin to the landscape in which they move; they seem, that is, to have a personal relation to Gaia, like mortals in an old myth; to be half man, half rock or tree. They are apotheoses of the power of natural environment. But Mr. Galsworthy's civilized people run down from town to hold hands amid the bracken because they feel that they are somehow justified by the fact of sap. It is all vague, of course; anything of that sort is bound to be vague. And if you are going to lean heavily on the cosmos, you want first to be sure that your *point d'appui* is not a spot where the cosmic force has chosen to manifest itself in vapor.

Mr. Galsworthy seems not to know in the least what he thinks about life. That state of maze may be satisfying to a hyper-sensitive soul, but it does not make for style. Besides, Mr. Galsworthy is old enough to have some idea as to what he does think about life. As far as one can make out, he thinks that most people are sensual, that everybody ought to be kind, and that there is a sustaining sanction for sex emotion in the fauna and flora of England. I do not know what Mr. Galsworthy's totem is; but it should be some small, defenceless bird. The snipe, perhaps.

Justice is said to have had a profound effect on English officials. Of that, one is glad; but one's quarrel with Mr. Galsworthy is that he will never think anything out. He inveighs against solitary confinement, which is a good thing to do; but he does not offer any substitute solution, which would be an even better thing to do. He sentimentalizes over dead pheasants and dead everything; but he gives you no suggestions as to what kind of laws to pass. He objects to existing divorce laws, but he does not come out into the open and say just what divorce laws, if any, he would propose to enact. It is not, apparently, either cowardice or expediency on his part; it is sheer inability to think constructively in any way. That is characteristic of many modern reformers: they want the bars let down here or there, but they never tell you in what spot the bars ought to be set up again. Beyond their gentle impulses, they are perfectly vague. It comes, I suppose, of trying to do your thinking with your heart instead of with your head. And in Mr. Galsworthy's case, the vagueness has permeated to the last recesses of his style. It is rhetorically accurate—"the English of a gentleman"—but it is jejune and spineless. It has become, you might say, a purely vegetarian meal. Only the graminivorous should read the later Galsworthy. And he will not rid himself of that fault by being increasingly explicit about sexual emotions. In fact, that never was his game.

I may seem to speak bitterly. I confess that I feel some bitterness. For I admired *The Man of Property* exceedingly, and looked to Mr. Galsworthy to carry on a great tradition of fiction. Instead of which, he has gone on backing, backing—farther and farther away from the Presence. Some people, I know, gave him up with *The Patrician* because, they said, it was straight Mrs. Humphry Ward. I gave him up forever with *The Freelands* because it was bad Mrs. Humphrey Ward; in fact, *The Coryston Family* was much better.

Now we come to our syndicate. With which shall we begin? It is hard to choose. Indeed, can you deal with them separately? For the outstanding fact is that they all write alike; that they deal in the same characters, the same backgrounds, and the same situations; and that they have the same point of view. They are like the Pléiade or the seven New Realists. Only they do not know it. At least, they

give no sign of intending to be several peas in
one pod. Yet you would almost say that none
of them had ever read anything but the works
of the others. Is there some master-mind
behind them, some literary Lloyd George or
Dr. Fu-Manchu, who assigns their tasks; who
says that Mr. Beresford, not Mr. Walpole,
shall write of Jacob Stahl, and that Mr. Mackenzie, not Mr. W. L. George, shall deal
with Michael Fane? And does Mr. Walpole
sneak off o' nights to Mr. Beresford and offer
to do some *Jacob Stahl* if Mr. Beresford
will take a few chapters of *Fortitude* off
his hands? Does Mr. Mackenzie write a page
of *A Prelude to Adventure* while Mr. Walpole takes a turn at *Sinister Street?* Who
does the murders? Is it Mr. Walpole or Mr.
Onions? Which one of them has been ap-
pointed to frequent the Empire? Does Mr.
George investigate female psychology for the
group? And what (but this I cannot even
guess) does Mr. D. H. Lawrence "cover"?

This may seem to be mere petulance, but
it is not. The chief value of fiction is, I take
it, to provide us with vicarious experience. A
great novelist who sticks to the truth is, above
all, informing. We enlarge our own world by
reading him. No one, in his own person, can
investigate all social *milieux* in all civilized
lands; and the big novels and the big plays
are text-books to the humanist. How much

intimate knowledge of France should we lose if we lost Balzac; how much intimate knowledge of England if we lost the great Victorians! Did we really, before the war, know anything about the Russian soul and temperament except what we got from the Russian novelists? Most of us get our India from Kipling. There are not wanting people to quarrel with Kipling's interpretation, even with his description; but the fact remains that a vast number of people know a few simple facts about Indian and Anglo-Indian life that they would never have known without him.

So that it is really not only the monotony, but the wilful extravagance, of the British syndicate that we complain of. Why waste half a dozen authors and a round score of novels to tell us the same thing in the same way? They do not even react differently to the same facts: they react precisely alike. Perhaps that is valuable as reinforcing and emphasizing the stated or implied opinion. But one has the sense that one is never going to learn anything more from any of them; and that is discouraging to the humanist, on vicarious experience bent. Perhaps one should except Mr. Walpole from that charge, to this extent: he gave us something new in *The Dark Forest*. In that book, at least, he made the Russians pleasanter than any of their own novelists (except possibly Turgenev) have succeeded in making them. But even so, if someone should tell us that Mr. Walpole, in the flesh, went to Russia to work with an ambulance corps, and that Mr. Beresford or Mr. Mackenzie wrote *The Dark Forest* from Mr. Walpole's notes, who could, from any internal evidence, deny it? If they were all Elizabethans, the scholars would still be wrangling over problems of their collaboration. Their novels would be like the Beaumont-Fletcher-Middleton-Rowley plays.

To begin with, there is always the same young man. Sometimes he has a university education, and then he is the hero of *Sinister Street* or *The Stranger's Wedding*; sometimes he has omitted the university, and then he is the hero of *Jacob Stahl* or *Fortitude*. He has usually decided, when we meet him, that there is nothing in religion; he is usually anxious to do something noble and unconventional; and sooner or later he nearly always encounters very seriously a young woman of, actually or potentially, light morals. Sometimes he is rich and meets her at the Empire; sometimes he is poor and meets her in the slums. Sometimes it is an accident, but usually he might fairly be said to be looking for her. For he is humanitarian, always; either by his gentle nature, or because socialistic arguments have got hold of him; and a good deal of space is always given up to sheer intellectual worrying. It *is* worrying—it seldom "gets" anywhere; and though Mr. Wells's people "worry" similarly, and do not always get anywhere, still, with Mr. Wells, you feel as if those men would, perhaps, sometime win through to a philosophy of their own. They go at it in a more mature fashion; and they possess themselves of information. There is something of the hard scientific temper in his men. They are more apt to have got their humanitarianism out of a laboratory than out of their first sight of Piccadilly Circus at night. Mr. Wells's men, when they are likable at all, are likable for some intellectual quality in them, for their attitude to ideas. When the syndicate's men are likable, it is for sheer pity, because they are such helpless young fools.

One expects every one in fiction, nowadays, to be an egotist; but one does sometimes sigh for the old days when an egotist knew enough to be polite. No one, I think, could feel any affection for Jacob Stahl; but it is possible to feel affection for Michael Fane, though it is perfectly impossible to feel him important, except as a householder always is important. Perhaps the most charming thing one remembers in any of these novels (they do not abound in charm) is the description of Oxford undergraduate life in *Sinister Street*. And it leads to—what? Michael's conscientious and pathetic progress among prostitutes and ruf-

fians. Luckily, he does not, in the end, marry
Lily; but he is saved from it by mere accident.
There was no reason to suppose that destiny
would play on his side.

This excursion into the underworld has become, in English fiction, almost as much *de
rigueur* for a young gentleman as the grand
tour used to be. Sometimes it is curiosity that
urges him; but it is more apt to be a kind of
humanitarian sympathy. The adventure is not
new: one remembers, after all, Richard Feverel. But the temper in which it is taken is
new. Richard was a chivalrous young fool;
but then Mrs. Mount was something out of
the ordinary. He did not, at first, dream what
she was; and when he found out, she was able
to lure him to think well of her. These young
gentlemen we are considering do not have to
be lured to think well of the young women
they altruistically encounter. They know before they meet them what they are going to
be. They cultivate them because they are that,
or are obviously going to be that. They prefer
the girl of the lower classes; prefer marriage
with her or free love with her, as the case
may be. They find her more interesting, just
as a settlement-worker finds the slums more
interesting. The difference between them and
the settlement-worker is that they are not out
to convert her to religion or even to better
manners. They are perfectly naïve in their

refusal to perceive differences. They have a
preconceived notion to the effect that there
are no differences; and to that notion they
often sacrifice themselves. Sometimes they sacrifice the girl.

You see, they do not think much of marriage, these young men. Jacob Stahl insists on
going off to a solitary cottage with Betty Gale,
unblessed. (Of course, he does have a wife in
the background.) He never quite forgives her
for wanting to be a legal wife. Though, char-
acteristically enough, by the time she has reconciled herself to the irregularity (as any
decent woman would have somehow to do, if
she were going to endure it) his wife dies,
and he insists on Betty's marrying him so that
they can have children. Ann Veronica over
again! But, indeed, Mr. Beresford has it in
for marriage anyhow. I know of nothing more
pathetic in modern fiction than the way Dick
Lynneker, brought up among gentlefolk, successful in his own career, in love with a girl
of his own class, has to cast about in his
mind for some way of squaring that conventional situation with his radicalism. Up to that
time, his only chance has been in approving of
his sister's elopement with the village carpenter. Now he is in love himself, and there is no
obstacle, social or financial, to his happiness.
But he has not protested against convention
all his young life, only to sit down and be

comfortable now in a conventional situation. Listen:

" 'I never tried to fight against my love for you, dear, after that first day at Oakstone,' he went on. 'I hadn't ever cared before for anyone like this. I've never had any sort of love-affair. And now, I want . . . .'

"She clung to him eagerly. 'What do you want, darling? she asked, and then added in-consequently, 'I feel such a little thing.'

"He drew her down to her knees and knelt before her in the darkness. 'I want our love to be all our own. I don't want it talked about and stared at. If we get married, it must be as quietly as possible—and it must be after-wards, if you know what I mean, dear? That legal business isn't for us at all; it's only a kind of registration. Our love hasn't anything to do with anyone else. We must make our vows without witnesses. Do you know what I mean, dear? Don't you feel like that, too?'

"He felt her heart throbbing violently against his; and they clung to each other like two frightened children. There, in the stillness and the darkness, the world had vanished and they were alone; and afraid; and yet passion-ately desirous to draw closer together.

" 'Oh! Dickie, I do love you so,' she whis-pered, as she put her lips to his."

Mr. Beresford never tells us whether or not Dick put his idea through. Sybil was the niece of a bishop. But then, Mr. Beresford made her. Perhaps Dick succeeded. The implication certainly is that he was going to succeed.

Now, I honestly think that pathetic. Not nearly so shocking as it is pathetic. For the author is looking for the realities of life in the wrong place. Every lover knows the sense of shrinking from a public ceremony. I doubt if any two people deeply in love with each other would choose, for their own sakes, a "wedding." Dick Lynneker need not think that his great idea is new. But look at the mad egotism of it! Take it that the legal or the ecclesiastical ceremony is merely a heavy price that one has to pay. Is that happiness not worth paying for? Generations of lovers have thought that it was. Suppose, even, that you think it not so much too heavy as the wrong kind of payment—something unjustly, shamelessly exacted of you, that should never have been exacted at all; a sort of Oriental "squeeze." Other lovers, in other times, have had a kindred sense of desecration; but they have realized that society, from its point of view, had a right to demand of them this public acknowledgment. They have realized, too, that no public act of this kind could really touch or affect their private sense of their private sacrament.

These modern folk are neither unselfish

enough to make their little salute to organized society cheerfully, nor strong enough to realize that the merely conventional tribute cannot hurt their private sanctities. There is no such unselfishness or strength possible to a person like Dick Lynneker. If we must face free love, we must face it, I suppose. But nothing in heaven or earth need make us face a compromise like Dick's. Defy all ritual and symbolism if you must. But, for sheer topsy-turviness, commend me to his notion of insisting on the consummation's preceding, instead of following, the ceremony! There is quite as much superstition in one order of things as in the other. Dick Lynneker is bound, quite as much as his family, by prejudices. After all, the black mass is only the real mass reversed.

I have dwelt on this instance because it seems to me typical, in its way, of the work of the whole group of English novelists. Except for Mr. Arnold Bennett, who seems to be satisfied with the mean and low-minded people of whom he feels that the world consists, they are all protesting. But they have nothing to suggest. When their own fitful attempts to set things straight result in failure or disaster, they blame the *status quo*. It never occurs to them to blame their own way of going about the business of changing things. A little study of history or even of sociology would teach them what not to waste their time on. But their only use for the past is to "curse it out." "Les grands-pères ont toujours tort." Yet they themselves go down like ninepins, knocked over by the same forces that, for a few thousand years at least, have been antagonizing the idealism and altruism of men. As I said before, one has some sympathy with Mr. Wells; for his people (his men, at least, since he does not think much better of women than does Arnold Bennett) are trying to inform themselves, trying to think it all out in terms of reason. The syndicate is not trying to think anything out. It rests content with replying to every affirmation of history: "You lie." That is not argument: it is the mere sticking out of tongues. The conventionally accepted thing *must* be wrong; and that is all there is to it.

Take the matter of their whole attitude to sex—which is, by and large, the question they are most preoccupied with. A certain person, a scholar and a gentleman, was pointing out to me, the other day, the accuracy of Chaucer's treatment of Troilus. Troilus lets Cressida go, not because he does not love her passionately, but because the chivalrous code demands it of him, demands that he should protect her reputation. Pandar cannot move him from his knightly duty. If ever a hero loved exuberantly, it was Troilus. Yet the inhibition works. Chaucer knew what he was talking about. Whereas, as my interlocutor went on to say, with these contemporary authors, the lack of inhibition seems to be the index of emotion. They ask you to take lawlessness for depth of feeling. The decorously behaved, according to them, are only the passionless. That is plain bad psychology. For if love is the real thing, it takes perpetually into account the duty to the beloved. Love will bring out the scruples of a comparatively unscrupulous person. No real lover wants to put the beloved "up against" anything disagreeable. And this being brave for someone else is not a natural expression of love. You may be brave to the rack and the gridiron for yourself; but being vicariously brave to the rack and the gridiron is a mean, modern kind of courage. Suppose you do not believe in the social order: the social order, none the less, is powerful enough to make a decent man want its approval for the woman he loves. He does not wish to have her inconvenienced—not if he loves her.

But the woman who does not wish to run up against the social order gets scant sympathy from the modern British hero. She ought to want to run counter to it; and if he has anything to say about it, she will jolly well have to. I do not know how other people feel about Betty Gale, but I am exceedingly sorry for her. I am sufficiently sorry for the girl who married Mr. Onions's murderer, the hero of *The Debit Account* and *In Accordance with the Evidence.* I am even sorry for Pauline in *Plashers Mead;* though, frankly, I think Mr. Mackenzie is fairer to his characters than any of the others. These young women (I am speaking, you see, at the moment, of the respectable ones) have such selfish, cantankerous, and muddle-headed gentlemen to deal with!

Our authors do succeed in making their conventional folk disagreeable. That is, they make the hero acutely perceptive of the conventional vices. But if ever there was a case of the beam and the mote! Look at a fair list of them: the hero of *The Invisible Event,* of *The Strangers' Wedding,* of *Round the Corner,* of *Plashers Mead,* of *The Debit Account.* Was there ever a more vaporing bunch of egotists anywhere? A great deal of fun has been poked at the heroes of the romantic period: the Manfreds and Laras, the Heathcliffs and Rochesters. Their revolts against society have been jests for the critics to split their sides over, these fifty years. But they were dignified creatures in comparison, and they had far more sense of fact. They knew, for example, when they bucked society, what they were bucking. They knew the process was not going to be entirely comfortable, and they did not complain of discomfort, because they saw a reason why it should be made hot for them. They simply felt that they

[241]

had a *quid pro quo*. They had, as I have said
elsewhere, the Satanic charm; they had also
some of the Satanic logic. These heroes have
been, for many decades, considered the wildest travesties of humanity. But, indeed, they
are far more comprehensible than the young
men in the modern British novels. A young
woman in love with Lara might well expect
the worst; but at least she would know what
to expect. Lara would never have shilly-
shallied about among the conventions like
Dick Lynneker, or Capes, or Jacob Stahl,
changing his mind from chapter to chapter,
and never knowing precisely what he did want,
anyhow. Lara would have known what he
wanted and why. He would not even have
hesitated to attribute to himself an evil motive, if he had one. But none of these young
men would attribute to himself an evil motive.
Whatever they want must be right; and if
eventually they want the exact opposite, then
that must be right, too. The bewildered woman follows in their wake.

That is why, by and large, they are so
corrupting. Yes, more corrupting than the
effervescent geniuses of the nineties. You
might be shocked by Dorian Gray, or by
Aubrey Beardsley's gentlemen and ladies; but
you were never tricked into imagining that it
was "up to you" to look like an Aubrey
Beardsley drawing or to behave like Dorian

Gray. The shining lights of the nineties lived to *épater le bourgeois*—and they did it. On the whole, that was greatly to the credit of *le bourgeois*. People who would rather die than show themselves *épatés* (there are always a lot of such folk) were very entertained. I dare say some of these authors and poets did harm in their day. But they did not do it by deluding the public into thinking that they were virtuous: they did it by being witty at the expense of virtue. Our novelists are not witty at the expense of virtue (or at the expense of anything else, be it said in passing). They perform all their antics in the very name of virtue. They are right, and everyone else is wrong.

Now the *révolté* with a programme we can endure, for we have often, during the muddled history of civilization, had to endure him. Sometimes he does a lot of damage; sometimes he does a lot of good. The point is that, in either case, his emotional force has been at the service of his programme. The trouble with these people is that they have no programme. They are *révoltés* because they are dissatisfied or in hard luck, and they hit wildly. They have not the brains to think anything out. Our friends of the nineties thought that nothing was sacred—except, perhaps, beauty. These folk know nothing about beauty—even Mr. Galsworthy, who may set you down on a hillside to look at a lovely landscape, and leave you there for several pages, but who spends his time during those pages in infecting that natural loveliness with notions of agrarian reform. The only thing that is sacred to these young folk is their own impulses; which makes them about as satisfactory to deal with as the wild gun in *Quatre-Vingt-Treize*. Since their own impulses chop and change—and are always sacred— you can do nothing except express perfect confidence in their temperaments. You are not to know them by their fruits; you are to judge them by their good intentions—for which you must take their own word.

Nor are they "ineffectual angels." If they only were! They are guilty of a lot of very ignoble impulses, and proceed often to gratify them. So did the romantic hero-villains, you may say. Ah, but here is the difference. The romantic hero-villains were proud, sometimes, of their sin; but they called it sin, even while they boasted of it. So did the æsthetes of the nineties. If it had not been sin, there would have been no fun in it. A very lamentable point of view, doubtless; but less dangerous to society than the contemporary mode. For while you still call it sin, you are accepting the categories, if not the judgments, of society. You will not hurt society much while you accept its categories. What these young men and young women do is to call anything virtuous that they happen to want to do. They have not even the logic of Satanists, perceiving evil and preferring it. The thing that is evil is the thing that makes them suffer; the thing that is good is the thing that pleases them. When free love is convenient, free love, only, is virtuous; marriage becomes virtuous the moment marriage becomes convenient. As you never know when obstacles are going to appear or disappear—as convenience is often in the hands of mere fortuitous fate—there is no test left. You must, I repeat, have blind faith in their temperaments. I do not think this is too hard a saying.

As for the women who match and mate with the men: they do not give us much more hope. They are, to speak plainly, an unlovely lot. You may be as sorry as you like for them, but pity is not praise. Mr. Wells's women are too apt to be selfish and treacherous; Mr. Bennett's opinion is evidently that no woman can be decent unless she is a fool—like Constance, say, in *The Old Wives' Tale*. (I know there is Alice Challis; but I fancy Alice is only a symbol of what every man wants and never gets.) And look, for a moment, at the women described by the syndicate. They are cheap: hard without being strong; cold without being pure; sentimental without being kind. There is the

sensual type—Madeline Paignton, the aristocratic wanton, or Lily Haden, who cannot be
continent for a few weeks, even for the sake
of wealth and a husband; there is all the crew
of light women among whom the heroes make
their humanitarian progress. There is the
intellectual (God save the mark!) type: the
heroine of *Gray Youth,* or even Rachel Beaminster, whose mental energy all goes into
revolt. If Mr. Walpole had made the Duchess
of Wrexe a human being, in whose reality we
could believe, we might have more sympathy
with Rachel's spiteful traffickings with the
family ne'er-do-well. But we should have to be
far sunk in fetishism to believe in the Duchess; she is a mere Mumbo-Jumbo; and her
family seems about as intelligent as the first
circles of Dahomey. Compare her, for an
instant, with Lady Kew. No, a tyranny like
that is an invented tyranny; it has nothing to
do with life. The Duchess of Wrexe (to bor-
row a term from the anthropologists) has no
mana at all. Rachel's revolt is absurd; and
simply shows up Rachel as a very disagreeable and headstrong person. True, there is
always something to make their revolts absurd. They seem not to be dealing with facts
at all, these young people; probably because
they are all sentimentalists, and for a sentimentalist a delusion is as good as a fact, any
day. A wicked giant is, by definition, anything

you happen to be tilting at—even if in real life he is a windmill.

You may say that two facts these characters do often deal with: poverty and the sex instinct. Yes, they are sometimes poor, and have a hard time. But they have just as hard a time when they are not poor. Poverty is not the root of all evil, logically exposed as such, as it so often is in the work of George Gissing. Not one of this group of authors has ever achieved the cumulative, inevitable tragedy of *New Grub Street*, for example: a far better indictment of some of the ills of the social order than all this modern mouthing. Indeed, not one of them is able to make anything seem inevitable. If they would only let the indictment be pitiless and let it stand; let us draw our own conclusions! And as for poverty, have you noticed that even when these young men are as poor as the hero of Mr. Onions's trilogy, they get over it? They never end in poverty. Yet their grievances are not disposed of when they become rich. By that time, they are worried about something else. They have the complaining habit. Rich or poor, married or unmarried, they are always, one foresees, going to complain. These authors convince one that their Utopia would be a hell on earth. They cannot reason; they cannot even dream convincingly. They are in a state of pitiful intellectual poverty—or, at least, penuriousness; for, if they have wealth, they certainly do not distribute it.

The sex instinct is, on the whole, their long suit. I do not think there is much more to be said about their treatment of it. They have not painted for us a nobler, or a more romantic, or a more passionate love between man and woman, than have some of their predecessors. I cannot see that these novelists give us anything new in the way of human information —except, perhaps, just one thing.

That one thing can best be described as a new theory—no, not a theory, a kind of Futurist presentment—of human types. There are just two possible things to do with the heroes and heroines of the new school; either to say that, as human beings, they do not exist; or to assume that they do exist and to lament the fact. The kinder, I believe, is to say that they do not exist. It is also the easier conclusion. For they are not consistent with themselves; they pass kaleidoscopically from one state of being to its opposite; as mortals, they are incalculable, and as literary creations they are unconvincing. "I don't believe there's any sich a person," is the natural reply to their presented cases. The authors have not the power of assuring us of the real existence of their characters. Life is not in them. If it is not a fault of vision, then it is a fault of technique. I have spoken of the

complete unreality of the Duchess of Wrexe;
but she is no more unreal than Dick Lynneker, or the hero of Mr. Onions's trilogy.
You can believe in far viler and wickeder
people, if you must; you can believe in Moll
Flanders or Carker or Long John Silver.
It is not moral but intellectual squeamish-
ness that makes it difficult to accept them.
Psychologically speaking, they are freaks in
side-shows. Mr. Bennett presents us with a
whole gallery of ignoble folk; but one is inclined to believe in some of them, at least.
Indeed, one is inclined to believe, thanks to
Mr. Bennett, that the Five Towns are almost
entirely populated with such (which may be
hard on the Five Towns, but that is Mr. Bennett's look-out). The syndicate has not Mr.
Bennett's technique.

Yet this is just where the very fact of the
syndicate gives one pause. Since there are so
many novelists in England doing precisely the
same kind of inconsistent, unconvincing, un-
lovable person, there may well be some genuine type that they are trying to describe.
Almost never, it seems to me, do they "get it
across"; but there must be people wandering
about the English landscape who have given
the syndicate the idea. We hardly believe that
their portraits are accurate; for their portraits are not psychologically possible. But
one comes to believe in prototypes. The syndi-

cate would not all, at a given signal, have
gone off their heads in exactly the same way.
They must have some warrant in fact. If the
prototypes of Jacob Stahl and of Dick Lynneker, of Rachel Beaminster and of the heroine of *Gray Youth* exist, these books are,
in a sense, a portent. The Five Towns might
be responsible for Hilda Lessways, but the
Five Towns are not responsible for the girl
in *Gray Youth*. One does not feel that the
syndicate gives one more than circumstantial
evidence, but of that, there is an almost over-
whelming amount. This is depressing. Perhaps, eventually, Mr. Compton Mackenzie
will resign from the syndicate and really tell
us something. At present he too is bound by
their conventions. But in *Plashers Mead,* tire-
some as it is with the reiterant egotism of
half-fledged youth, he does "get it across."
Certain people whose opinion is worth much
more than mine, tell me that Mr. Walpole
has got it across in *The Dark Forest. I*
must admit, in my own case, the strict limita-
tions of western Europe: it will take more
than Mr. Walpole to make Russians credible
to me. He seems to me no more plausible than
Dostoievsky, and far, far short of Turgenev.
And, after all, I am not sure that Nijinsky
is not a better expositor than either.

It has been much more difficult than I
dreamed, to deal with these gentlemen at all.

The work of one shifts and plays into the work of the other so maddeningly that it is hard, not only to treat of them individually, but to treat of them even as a group. You think you have a line on Mr. Walpole, and you find him melting into Mr. Beresford or Mr. Onions. Everyone knows what a miserable business a composite photograph is. No feature is really defined. These authors differentiate themselves just enough by detail of plot and setting and diction, to avoid a grand inclusive charge of plagiarism. You cannot say that one has filched a page from another, because there is no telling who began it. But I believe that, as far as style is concerned, if you inserted six consecutive pages written severally by the six of them, in any chapter of any book, no one would ever know the difference. Of course, you would have to allow for different names of characters, and some havoc might be played with continuity of plot—if there happened to be any plot in that chapter. But the style would, I am sure, stand the test. Mr. Mackenzie forces his vocabulary as the others do not (he prides himself, I fancy, particularly on the number of his metaphors for the moon); but apart from Mr. Mackenzie's occasional exoticism, they write alike. They have the same rhythms, the same sentence-structure, the same syntactical habits. It is clever, nervous writing, but it is not the grand style. They are not memorable: they do not stand out, any one of them, or any one of their works, as a mental experience. The only adventure to be got from them is to read them all, and then, forgetting (as you inevitably do) who is who and which is which, analyze the effect of the group. It is a hazy and perplexing effect—as I fear I have too meticulously said.

For in the long run, one's main feeling about the younger English writers is one of sheer disappointment. They have their reputation: people are always telling you that this one or that one is really important. I cannot believe that they are. As portrayers of life, they do not convince—a matter partly of muddle-headedness and partly of technique in the narrower sense. Moreover, they are dull. Mr. Bennett may not convince in the end, because in the end one becomes aware of his moral myopia; but he is not usually dull. He writes better than they do—that is what it comes to. If there were only one of them, we might put up with him; but how can we put up with six of him? There is not time. As for their attack on convention, whatever it may be, they will have to do it better to get any serious attention paid to them. You need seasoned troops to attack that fortress—or at least bigger guns. The only person who thinks that anything, no matter what, is better than the *status quo,* is the anarchist. Most of us are not anarchists; and while most of us are willing to have things improved, if necessary, at our own expense, we want some assurance that they will be improved. And if we must make blind experiments—as the reformers all want us to—let us at least know the object of the experiment. These writers do not seem to know what they would like to achieve if they could.

What they chiefly breed in one is hopelessness. If this is the best that England can do for us in the way of fiction, we must either encourage our native product, or eschew fiction and take to "serious" reading. These men are too dull. The time is ripe, once more, I believe, for a few big picaresque novels: something in the mode of the *Satyricon,* and *Gil Blas,* and *Huckleberry Finn.* For I do not think that people will put up forever with being bored—especially as they are not boring us in the interests of virtue.

To be sure—though it is some time since I began this essay—I have still not read D. H. Lawrence.

THE REMARKABLE RIGHTNESS
OF RUDYARD KIPLING

IT looks Chestertonian as I write it. As if a
world of concrete things were to be gathered into the titular abstraction; or as if
Kipling's rightness were presently to be proved
remarkable in that it is all wrong.

And yet, I think, Chesterton or no Chesterton—where is he, by the way?—I mean
precisely what I have set down: Rudyard Kipling's remarkable rightness. Right, because
time has sustained him against scoffers; remarkable, because no one originally expected
that particular kind of rightness from him.

This is not to be a discursive or an exhaustive discussion of Kipling's utterances on plan-
etary or even racial questions. I have not
annotated his complete works with his "rightness" in mind. Indeed, to treat him exhaustively would be a very difficult task; for the
sum of his wisdom is made up, not of a few
big "works," but of an infinite number of
significant brevities. My only excuse for dealing with him at all is that I have lived a long
time with the prose and verse of Kipling, and
that my knowledge of him has reached what
Henry James called the point of saturation. I

will not pretend that I have read every word he has ever printed in the Allahabad *Pioneer* or even in the London *Times*; but I know him very well. I belong to the generation that took its Kipling hard. My friends who are five years older or five years younger never took him quite so hard as that. They knew other gods.

Rudyard Kipling, in his later life, has suffered under two great disadvantages: his insistence on a political point of view which was unpopular, and the gradual diminishing of his flow of masterpieces. The dullest people will tell you smartly that he is "written out"; the cleverest will tell you that he was precocious, but always cheap, if not vulgar. Perhaps someone will fling "The Female of the Species" at you. This paper is not to be a catalogue of Kipling's virtues, nor yet of his achievements. But I should like you to consider with me for a few moments that little volume of verse, *The Five Nations*. I take *The Five Nations* purposely, for it is the Kipling of *The Five Nations* that I mean. Not the better known Kipling of the *Barrack-Room Ballads* or *The Seven Seas*. But supremely the Kipling I refer to.

Two things changed the Kipling we first knew: renewed residence in England, and the Boer War. Of course, he was always an imperialist; he always loved Lord Roberts—as

[255]

long ago as the *Plain Tales,* when Kipling
was at once younger and cleverer than anyone
else. But he saw these things, then, from the
angle of India; he was an imperialist only in
embryo. He cared more for the British army
—in red—than for the British navy; and
Anzacs were not within his vision.

Then—by devious paths—he returned to
England; and England held him as it held the
man and the woman in "An Habitation Enforced." The Boer War came; and *The Five
Nations* tells how he reacted. He has gone
on very consistently from that day, developing,
but never swerving from the path of his conviction. England did not listen to him: the
Liberals of the first decade of the twentieth
century did not propose to listen to anyone
who wrote short stories for the sake of the
plot, and verse for the sake of a Tory idea.
They were much too serious in Great Britain,
in those days, to hearken to Rudyard Kipling.
And, so far as I know, neither Lord Roberts
nor Kipling ever said, "I told you so."

Yet listen to "The Lesson":

It was our fault, and our very great fault—and now we
    must turn it to use;
We have forty million reasons for failure, but not a
    single excuse!

How one has heard that rough-and-ready
poem reviled—in the early nineteen-hundreds!
Even now one recalls abusive editorials in

American newspapers about the poem which mentioned

> . . . the flannelled fools at the wicket . . . the muddied oafs at the goals.

"Oblige me by referring to the files." I remember those taunting comments very well. Not an editor but was so sane that he could make his little mock of Kipling as an extremist. But if you will get out *The Five Nations* and read "The Islanders" through soberly, you will curse those editors for fools. "Preparedness" is so familiar to us all now, not only as a word but even as an idea, that we can hardly believe intelligent people were calling a man names fifteen years ago for stating axioms. We are always thinking the days of Galileo are over. But they are not; they never will be; the human race instinctively and always has it in for Galileo. Kipling could get an audience for tales and ballads and jungle-books; but the moment he tried to speak nationally, he could not get an audience. Even now, they would rather read H. G. Wells.

> Do ye wait for the spattered shrapnel ere ye learn how
> a gun is laid?
> For the low red glare to southward when the raided
> coast towns burn?
> (Light ye shall have on that lesson, but little time to
> learn.)"

"Yes, thanks," came the sarcastic answer from all the wise British millions; "we jolly

well *do* wait." And they "jolly well" did; and
a dozen years later it all came true, and their
sarcasm was put where it belonged. That is, if
they had the sense to see it.

> Will ye pray them or preach them, or print them, or
> ballot them back from your shore?
> Will your workmen issue a mandate to bid them strike
> no more?

Well: it very nearly came to that. But I suggest that you re-read "The Islanders." I cannot quote any more. Every word of "The
Islanders" is true to make one weep; and it
was the storm-centre of *The Five Nations*.
How many thousands of people felt that, in
writing "The Islanders," Kipling had destroyed
his own reputation! Doubtless the Germans
would have felt the same way about "The
Parting of the Columns"; though, if they had
read it and had taken the trouble to believe it,
it would have saved them a good many millions spent in propaganda. But the Germans
were quite as stupid as the British public.

There has been more than one reason, as I
have said, for the waning of Kipling's popu-
larity. In the first place, he does not give us so
many good stories as once, in the full flush of
his genius, he did. That is a perfectly legitimate reason. Then, too, he has had an unlucky trick of seeing ahead. When "The Edge
of the Evening" was first published (in 1913),

it passed for hysteria. Only "fools" believed in German spies—in 1913. But there are other causes more insidious and more potent. He stands, not only politically for the highest type of Toryism—at least, one fancies he does—but for a lot of other outdated things: pious attachment to the soil; romantic love, enduring, clean outside and in; the beauty of childhood and the bitterer beauty of parenthood; patriotism unshrinking and unashamed; loathing of the mob and the mob's madness and meanness; the continuity of the English political tradition, from Magna Charta down; religious toleration; scrupulous perception of differences between race and race, type and type; the White Man's Burden. And I doubt if, even now, he is an ardent believer in Woman Suffrage.

Almost any one of these attitudes would have been enough to damn him with the British democracy. One quite understands that *The Five Nations* would not have been Mr. Lloyd George's *vade mecum*. One perfectly sees why Mr. Asquith, following the usual tradition, passed Kipling over for the Laureateship in favor of a gentleman whom few people had heard of and no one could read. ("The Widow at Windsor" probably shocked Balliol as much as it shocked Queen Victoria.) No Kipling-lover, for that matter, particularly wanted Kipling to be Laureate. One even real-

izes—though this time with amusement—why
he is *persona non grata* to the "brittle intellectuals who crack beneath a strain." The
intellectuals say that he is good at times for
children, and often for the vulgar, and take
their refuge in not taking him seriously. The
intellectuals have been Russianizing themselves, in these last years; and Kipling's
laughter at that phenomenon must have been
unholy. They could scarcely afford to feel
him remarkably right, it would prove them so
remarkably wrong.

As I say, one quite understands why the
gorged and flattered workingman, the demagogue, and the "brittle intellectual" have not
read him or listened to him; but it is none the
less a mystery that some one should not have
listened to him and seen that he was eminently
sane on many vital points. There is, after all,
no one living in England who writes so well,
who is so nearly master of the English language. But one has to conclude that his audience has made up its mind only to be amused
during a train-journey.

There was a merry little international cor-
respondence in 1914 or 1915 over "The Truce
of the Bear." What did Mr. Kipling say *now?*
It was all a great joke on him. People also
raked up "The Man Who Was." I believe
Mr. Kipling never replied to his humorous
questioners, or, if he did, it was to the effect

that a man, like a government, might change
his foreign policy with changing conditions.
Still, everybody was very much amused, and
for some reason (it can have been only his
unpopularity) very much pleased. Perhaps
they had not forgiven some of the other poems
in *The Five Nations,* and looked to dis-
credit Kipling by pitching on "The Truce of
the Bear" as they had once pitched on "The
Islanders." With Russia driving back the Teu-
tons on the eastern front, I do not see that
Kipling, as a patriot, could proceed to defend
his ancient position very loudly. But I do not
remember—here I speak under correction, for
his war-poems are very elusive—that even
since 1914 he has written of Russia as he has
written of France. And I have often wondered
if, in the last months, he has not taken a very
private comfort in his own refrain of years
ago:

Make ye no truce with Adam-zad, the bear that walks
    like a man.

He may at least feel that he was essentially
right about Russia, if incidentally wrong. If I
am not mistaken, "The Truce of the Bear"
was written on the occasion of the invitation
to the first Hague Conference. We took it that
it was the Tsar whom England was to mis-
trust. Very likely. But I cannot help believing
that Kipling had a private suspicion that the

Hague Conference was all tommy-rot. Which, obviously, it was, pragmatically judged. The sheer decency and competence of certain Russian generals did save the world in the first year of the war: let us never forget it. There never was a Russian steam-roller, but the Germans thought there was going to be one. Let us, as I say, never forget it. But for the last year, the Russian people has been behaving allegorically in the sense of the poem.

'When he stands up like a tired man, tottering near and
   near;
When he stands up as pleading, in wavering, man-brute
   guise. . . .

When he shows as seeking quarter, with paws like hands
   in prayer,
That is the time of peril—the time of the Truce of the
   Bear!'

Eyeless, noseless, and lipless, asking a dole at the door,
Matun, the old blind beggar, he tells it o'er and o'er;
Fumbling and feeling the rifles, warming his hands at
   the flame,
Hearing our careless white men talk of the morrow's
   game;

Over and over the story, ending as he began:—
'*There is no truce with Adam-zad—the bear that looks like
   a man!*'

I should be particularly sorry to say anything that German propagandists would like to have said. It is perfectly impossible for the average person to know what is the proper

and what the improper attitude to take to
Russia at the moment. Even those in high
places might be forgiven for being perplexed.
What the average person perceives is that the
Russians are behaving very much, and very
vividly, like "the bear that looks like a man."
Certainly they stood up at Brest-Litovsk "in
wavering, man-brute guise."

The only point of all which is that the folk
who made so merry, a few years ago, over
"The Truce of the Bear" had better find
another joke. One does not base the rightness
of Kipling on his merely having been a little
less ridiculous, in a given instance, than his
contemporaries wanted to think him.

I wonder, too—still as I turn the pages of
The Five Nations—if there is not a tonic
value today in the poem called "Sussex."

> God gave all men all earth to love,
>   But since our hearts are small,
> Ordained for each one spot should prove
>   Beloved over all;
> That, as He watched Creation's birth,
>   So we, in godlike mood,
> May of our love create our earth
>   And see that it is good.
>
> So one shall Baltic pines content,
>   As one some Surrey glade,
> Or one the palm-grove's droned lament
>   Before Levuka's trade.
> Each to his choice, and I rejoice
>   The lot has fallen to me
> In a fair ground—in a fair ground—
>   Yea, Sussex by the sea!

So to the land our hearts we give
Till the sure magic strike,
And Memory, Use, and Love make live
Us and our fields alike—
That deeper than our speech and thought,
Beyond our reason's sway,
Clay of the pit whence we were wrought
Yearns to its fellow-clay.

The windy internationalism to which we are so often invited, nowadays, to listen, would deny it—might even call it *"chauvinisme de clocher."* The reply is that people actually do feel as Kipling says they do. He has always tended to serve (in his own phrase) the God of Things as They Are. Granted, for the sake of argument, that it would be good for you to love all men and all countries alike, the fact remains that you do not. If that is your duty, most decent people do not perform their duty; their fathers did not, and their children will not. Even the most radical internationalists wish to substitute class-consciousness for patriotism—on the whole, a less enlightened chauvinism than the other. And, judging from the present war, they have not been able to pull even that off.

As for saying that one has the same sense of personal insult in seeing a foreign land invaded as in seeing one's own, that is nonsense. France has been the home of the spirit to many of us; the thought of an invaded France is of a bitterness hardly to be borne.

But though one has lived in it and loved it, one is not so angry, in the very depths of one, at Teuton occupation of France as one would be at Teuton occupation of one's own soil. I will not say what German invasion of my own New England would be to me. "Ten generations of New England ancestors" would rise up to curse the enemy. But even an invaded Oshkosh (and Oshkosh is a mere name to me) would be to me, an American, an even deadlier insult than an invaded Paris. I should take it more personally, I know. And if that can be so for us, in our far-flung, heterogeneous republic, what must be the case with the children of homogeneous France? If I know that I should feel that way about Oshkosh, what must the Kentish man feel about Kent, the Devonshire man about Devon, the Englishman about England? Did not all sane Americans between Bangor and San Diego react in precisely similar fashion to Herr Zimmermann's plans for Texas? I have never even been in Texas, but Texas belongs to me and I belong to it.

No: say what you please, geography is the great human science; it is more intimate than biology. And Kipling has had the sense to see it because he really knows something about the *genus homo*. It was a delightful phrase of the Frenchman's that charmed our youth— "the passion for the planet"; but are we not a

little undeceived now? Do we not at last realize that the only real "man without a country"
is the cosmopolite? If there be such a person.

I can almost hear someone quoting iron-
ically,

> But there is neither East nor West, border nor breed
> nor birth,
> When two strong men stand face to face, though they
> come from the ends of the earth.

That is very taking; and in a sense it is true,
thank Heaven. But I fancy Kipling would
want to modify it now. At least he would like
to write a foot-note containing a careful definition of the word "strong." It would not
apply to the average German.

Kipling was called, for many years, by the
pacifist-Liberals, a jingo. All imperialists were,
ex officio, jingoes. Some of these people have
got into their heads, by this time, the conception of a "preparedness" that makes for
peace, and realize the difference between a
real jingo and a man who wants to avert war
in the only way possible when a considerable
portion of the world remains militaristic. We
all know by this time that, if England had
been prepared in 1914, there would have been
no war in 1914; that, very probably, if Sir
Edward Grey had been empowered to say, at
the proper instant, that England would fight,
there would have been no war in 1914. Had

[266]

"The Army of a Dream" been there, the mailed fist would not have been shaken at the world. But that is ancient history. It is to be hoped that not every one who preached preparedness in the old days is now stigmatized as a jingo. If anyone still thinks of Kipling vaguely as a war-mad imperialist, let him read "The Settler":

> Earth where we rode to slay or be slain,
> Our love shall redeem unto life;
> We will gather and lead to her lips again
> The waters of ancient strife,
> From the far and fiercely guarded streams
> And the pools where we lay in wait,
> Till the corn cover our evil dreams
> And the young corn our hate.

That is not the accent of the dyed-in-the-wool jingo.

And here again—still out of *The Five Nations*—the "Half-Ballad of Waterval":

> *They*'ll never know the shame that brands—
> Black shame no livin' down makes white,
> The mockin' from the sentry-stands,
> The women's laugh, the gaoler's spite.
> We are too bloomin' much polite,
> But that is 'ow I'd 'ave us be . . .
> Since I 'ave learned at Waterval
> The meanin' of captivity.

Written at least fifteen years ago—and still, I fancy, the core of the matter. Certainly very

[267]

different from imperialistic-militaristic conceptions of the rights of prisoners as exemplified
by—Wittenberg, let us say.

All these later quotations go to show
merely that Kipling need not have been so
slanged for *The Five Nations,* since in much
of *The Five Nations* he has pretty well
expressed fundamental British feeling—as is
now, day by day, being proved. And—let us
face it squarely—fundamental British feeling
is on the whole the most decent on earth. As
Americans, we like to think that we share it.
No one, to be sure, paid much attention to the
poems just cited: they took it out in criticizing
things like "The Lesson," "The Islanders,"
and "The Old Men." Now we find that in
those much-execrated poems he told the simple
truth. Why not admit it? Admit, that is,
ungrudgingly, not only that he has been right
since 1914, but that he was right much earlier,
and that it is the other people who have had
to shift their point of view.

But policies—as well foreign as domestic—
have, from of old, made bitter enemies and
excited acrimonious controversy. No one could
have said anything worse about Kipling than
political folk in all the serious English reviews
were saying (before the war), all the time,
about their political opponents. You could
never take up one of those famous periodicals
without feeling that vitriol had been spilled in

your very presence. If there is a special rhetoric of vituperation, the English political article was its textbook. We milder Americans gasped. No Southern gentleman, on the floor of the Senate, ever went quite so far.

So we should expect Kipling to be called horrid names by those who disagreed with him politically, because that is English political manners. No one really minds, except as one has always resented the doom of Cassandra. What one does mind, what one does resent, is the judgment of the "intellectuals" on Kipling's general human knowledge. They seem to agree with Oscar Wilde that, in turning over the pages, "one feels as if one were seated under a palm-tree reading life by superb flashes of vulgarity. . . . From the point of view of literature Mr. Kipling is a genius who drops his aspirates. . . . He is our first authority on the second-rate, and has seen marvellous things through key-holes, and his backgrounds are real works of art." Even Henry James spoke of him tentatively, as a young man who had gone a long way before breakfast. Politics always make people see red; but the human emotions in general, people ought to be able to discuss amicably. And the intellectuals have never been willing to discuss Kipling at all. When he is dead, they will, of course. But at present they still consider him negligible.

Now no one—unless Rudyard Kipling him-

self—is less tempted than I to set Rudyard
Kipling up as "saint and sage," or to try to
establish a Kipling philosophy or a Kipling
cult. You may take a man seriously without
taking him religiously, I should hope. But the
intellectuals take other people religiously, not
to say seriously; and why Kipling is to be
forever relegated by our arbiters of taste to
the ranks of the frivolous or the hysterical or
the vulgar, passes the normal understanding.

Two demands can respectably be made of
a writer, in order that he should be taken
"seriously": that he should be to some extent
a master of style, and that he should have
sane and serious things to say about life. To
those who insist that Kipling is not a master
of English style, one has, really—now I come
to think of it—nothing to say. Especially as
many of them will tell you, with straight faces,
that Galsworthy, or Arnold Bennett, or someone else, *is* a master of style. Chiefly, it means
that they care so little about what he says that
they belittle his way of saying it. They persist
in taking a purely momentary point of view.
Kipling, I fancy, can afford to await the judgment of posterity. He is destined to become a
great English name.

There are probably several reasons for this
critical scorn. One is that he writes short
stories, and short stories are not yet so dignified as novels—unless the writer be Mau-

passant. Some of the critics have never read anything but the earliest Kipling. Largely, it is because they have not the faintest approximation to a Chaucerian or Shakespearean sense of life—life, good and bad, high and low, grave and gay—and they find no charm, no "distinction" in the blessed, common, earthy Englishness of the English scene. Most of all, they are uninterested in the very universality of the emotions and events he deals with: patriotism, love, childhood and parenthood, duty, and death. Nor have they much taste for laughter. As for tradition, they are so busy scrapping it, that they are not concerned with illustrations of its continuity and deathlessness.

I could get up a better brief for Kipling on the human score, if I were not making it a point of honor to stick to *The Five Nations.* For Kipling has gone on very much, even since then. *The Five Nations* deals particularly with the Boer War and reactions after the Boer War. His more explicitly "human" wisdom is not to be found there in greatest measure. Yet in some ways *The Five Nations* comes home to us just now more than other things, when we are in the midst of the very war which he therein prophesied.

Take the "Chant-Pagan." When the war is over, there will be some millions of Englishmen (to leave out the other Allies) who will come home singing that chant—if not literally, then in spirit. In fact, that is the most encouraging thing in all Kipling for the reformers—except that I do not believe the returned soldier will care much more for the English industrial paradise than for the "Squire an' 'is wife." Even old-age pensions and the abolition of great estates, and all the other articles of Lloyd George's faith, are not going to make him happy. He is going to know too much about real values. There is just a chance that, after having saved England in the field, he may save England at home. There will—God send!—be so many of him. No man can prophesy; and yet already, in America, one hears people wondering about our own boys, in the very sense of the "Chant-Pagan."

Naturally, as I say, the more personal human relations are not dealt with in *The Five Nations*. But there remains "The Second Voyage." I do not know that anything saner or wiser or more poignant has ever been written about that love between man and woman which is the bulwark of Occidental civilization. No one can deal more tenderly than Kipling with the idyll between boy and girl—look at "The Brushwood Boy." He can even deal convincingly with the great illicit love (though it is not a favorite theme of his)—witness "Without Benefit of Clergy" and the great paragraph in "Love o' Women." But the love that he most often treats is the love between

[272]

husband and wife: the love that is built on shared tears and laughter, on deep domestic sympathies and clean sex-attraction, the love that many waters cannot quench. In "The Second Voyage" he explicitly renounces all others; it expresses love, if you like, more or less according to the prayer-book. He sacrifices to the god of Romantic Marriage. If you choose to put it that way, there ain't a lady livin' in the land as he'd change for 'is dear old Dutch. Perhaps that is why they call him vulgar. Many of our "serious" contemporaries appear to resent any account of human relations that is both vitally human and essentially decent, because it leaves at one side their two preferred groups: the very sophisticated, and the criminal classes.

I suspect that one difficulty, for the more sincere, if still brittle, intellectuals, lies in the unconventional verse-forms which Kipling often affects. They can stand any amount of slang in prose, but they cannot endure it in verse. At least, they do not believe that "high seriousness" can wear such a garb. I dare say they would throw out even "The Second Voyage" on the score of unconventionality. Well: let them. I was going to quote some of it, but I am too out of temper with the intellectuals. They may read it for themselves. And probably none of the moderns would be able to endure the mention of "Custom, Reverence, and Fear." I give it up. But they need not think that Kipling's own education in the matter of sex-relations stopped with the Gadsbys.

To the mind of the serious Kipling-lover, the thing that grows more and more impressive is his universality. Perhaps it seems to some an unimportant list of allegiances that I have mentioned: "pious attachment to the soil; romantic love, enduring, clean outside and in; the beauty of childhood and the bitterer beauty of parenthood; patriotism unshrinking and unashamed; loathing of the mob and the mob's madness and meanness; the continuity of the English political tradition, from Magna Charta down; religious toleration; scrupulous perception of differences between race and race, type and type; the White Man's Burden." Many a man has had a tablet in Westminster Abbey for a lesser creed. And almost no one has sought his wisdom and his delight in so many places or so many classes of society. Engineers, subalterns, ladies of the manor, cockney privates, Hindu bearers, Boer farmers, half-caste Portuguese nursemaids, Gloucester fishermen, bank clerks, reporters, young English children, German scientists, law lords, public-school boys, lamas, pilots, children of the zodiac, even the beast-folk of the jungle—what a Shakespearean welter, and, humanly speaking, what a Shakespearean result! It is the "good gigantic smile o' the

brown old earth." And the far-flung adventure
has brought Kipling back to a very simple but
not too easy code. At least, one cannot say
that he sticks by the most English of English
traditions because he has never seen anything
else. He has had room and chance to choose.
He has ended by being very orthodox, not to
say conventional, about the fundamental human duties; and he reads history with a canny
eye. But I do not think anyone can accuse Kipling of being a stick-in-the-mud. "With the
Night Mail" does not look so Jules Verne-ish
now as it did when it was printed. Perhaps
some day we shall even have to give the benefit of the doubt to the later "flight of fact"
called "As Easy as A. B. C." Though I admit
that that is going far.

Just there, I did leave *The Five Nations*
for the moment; but it is impossible to mention "As Easy as A. B. C." and not also quote
some of "MacDonough's Song."

> Whether the People be led by the Lord,
>   Or lured by the loudest throat;
> If it be quicker to die by the sword
>   Or cheaper to die by vote—
> These are the things we have dealt with once,
>   (And they will not rise from their grave)
> For Holy People, however it runs,
>   Endeth in wholly Slave.
>
> Whatsoever, for any cause,
>   Seeketh to take or give

Power above or beyond the Laws,
  Suffer it not to live!
Holy State or Holy King—
  Or Holy People's Will—
Have no truck with the senseless thing.
  Order the guns and kill!

  Saying—after—me:—

'Once there was The People—Terror gave it birth;
  Once there was The People and it made a Hell of
  Earth.
Earth arose and crushed it. Listen, O ye slain!
Once there was The People—it shall never be again!'

Easy enough to see why Kipling is not popular. Yet Kipling is by no means the only person who is warning us that mob-rule may come and sweep away our institutions. Most people who fear that event are doing their best to ingratiate themselves with the mob before it wholly loses its temper. I confess that—politics apart, and as a mere matter of dignity—it is a comfort to hear some man speak in another spirit and sense than that of craven conciliation. I have not quoted from "MacDonough's Song" because I think it is a great poem; but because it is perhaps the most nakedly, blatantly "unpopular" thing Kipling has ever written. There it is, openly admitted, in all its offensiveness—his greatest crime. Damn him for it if you feel inclined, but confess that to write as uncompromisingly as that is better manners than to have loathing or fear in your heart and honey on your lips. "We reason with them in Little Russia," says Dragomiroff in "As Easy as A. B. C." Well, it looks as if, several generations ahead, that might still be the method in Little Russia. The story was written in 1912.

The Five Nations ends with the "Recessional," which preceded the Boer War by three years. And there is nothing to add to the "Recessional," even now; except that Germany needs to read it, at present, more than England does. All that I have meant to do is to point out that Kipling was right about preparedness, right about the Colonies, right about Germany, right about Russia, right about the Boers, right about Kitchener, right about demagogues and "labor," right about the elderly politicians, right about the decent British code, right about patriotism and the human heart—right about love; and that for all those things (except the last) he was slanged as if he were wrong. In political matters, "thought is free," with us, at least. But in the matter of literary criticism, it seems a pity not to realize the worth and distinction of the few people we have who possess either. I have been told that Kipling still sells better than any other author in America. When I think of Harold Bell Wright, I hope, for the credit of America, that it is true. Perhaps the attitude of the intellectuals is mere snobbishness, which cannot consent to think a best-seller literature. But, as I say, it is a pity that the greatest living master of English style (for Conrad's is a restricted field) should not be confessed to as such by the few who still profess to care about style. One would not mind so much if they did not commend such a lot of third-rate stuff.

I am glad that Kipling himself has the vulgar consolation of royalties. He has, to be sure—I repeat—the disadvantage of telling the truth prematurely. If we have just about caught up with *The Five Nations*—well, let us hope that the argument from analogy will not work in this case: that we shall never have to catch up with "As Easy as A. B. C."; that that, at least, may not be an instance of his remarkable rightness. For it does not make one happy about the immediate future.